DEDICATION

To Virgil Cooper, whose wit, wisdom, and computer legerdemain have brought me and my company into the present century. Everybody should have such a saint patiently solving their daily devilments. This book is his, with eternal gratitude.

TABLE OF CONTENTS

Introduction, 7

1. The premise, 10
2. Publishing as usual: the standard publisher, 12
3. The alternative: a self-published book to tightly-targeted markets, 21

TARGETING

4. Finding, defining, and qualifying the target market, 26
    Example, 31
5. Finding and defining a specific market need, 42
    Example, 45

CUSTOMIZING

6. Meeting that need through a book: checking, measuring, and fitting, 50
    Example, 57
7. Meeting that need through other information dissemination means, 64
    Example, 74
8. Determining where and how to sell the book to the targeted market, 81
    Example, 84
9. Identifying the promises the book's promotion must make and what the promotional tool must include, 87
    Example, 93
10. Evaluating potential profit against working capital, 98
    Example, 105
11. Picking a title, creating testing tools, and testing your book — twice! 112
    Example, 120
12. Gathering information and writing the book, 131
    Example, 140
13. Producing the book — or having it produced, 146
    Example, 153
14. Promoting and selling the book, 157
    Example, 166

EXPANDING

15. Converting the book into more books, 181
    Example, 184
16. Sharing the information by other dissemination means, 188
    Example, 189

Bibliography, 196
Index, 197

INTRODUCTION

The title of this book sounds like the true path to penury. Self-publishing is hard enough, but to tightly-targeted markets? More work and greater risk to sell to fewer people?

You're in for a real surprise!

It may be the best kept secret in the book publishers' trove that true fortunes and sweet futures can come from pinpointing and helping meet specific needs of reachable markets. Best yet, in this arena the small publisher can beat the giant at his own game every time!

The title of this book describes its contents precisely: how one self-publishes to tightly targeted markets. Yet the book does much more.

Beyond explaining the concept, it presents a system that will take you step-by-step through the process, and shows as it tells with examples that you can follow or from which you can extrapolate to publish your own book and cull your own rewards.

Moreover, this process greatly reduces the risks and costs of self-publishing while increasing your profits, and the certainty of them.

And the book talks about a philosophy, a way of sharing information.

It shows how, as a self-publisher, you can use your book as the core of a larger market penetration through which you can sell the same or related information more often and more widely.

That is, it suggests that as important as your book is, the expertise that you display about its subject is more important still. That by sharing that expertise, through additional books or other information dissemination means, you can create an empire that could multiply your income mightily as you help others meet their needs.

But I'm getting ahead of myself. The next chapter begins the fleshing out of these promises.

Self-Publishing to Tightly-Targeted Markets mostly talks about marketing, then writing, then expanding the marketing again, which is what all publishers do. And while the process focuses on books, the concept and many of the steps can usually be applied to any other means of information dissemination, such as articles, speeches, seminars, audio or video tapes, newsletters, or consulting.

I call it the "TCE process" because the three key elements are Targeting, Customizing, and Expanding. A section of the book is devoted to each element. But first I explain the concept in greater detail, show how standard publishing is inappropriate for almost all tightly-targeted publishing, and how the alternate, the self-publishing path, is ideal for this purpose. Finally, a list of "other sources and guides" is included to lead you to specific, applicable information about the steps you must follow to self-publish and successfully market.

This book is about book writing and publishing because, of the many means, I know it best and I most want to share a new process about it with you. It is my seventh book. The first was sought by the major publisher in my field but I decided to publish it myself. (They later included the second edition of that book, plus my fourth book, as top choices for their book club.) The decision to self-publish was the brightest thing I have done in years. It gave me an opportunity to learn about the full spectrum of publishing from an independent yet involved perspective. Which, in turn, led to the TCE process and this book.

The TCE process is neither a panacea nor publishing salvation. It simply will not work for some books, as I will explain. Yet it will work for many more, most of which would never be published by the standard houses and therefore would probably never be written and see print.

That is my greatest motivation for writing these pages. I am naive enough to believe that we can have a perfect human world on this earth and that one of the keys to its creation is knowledge shared as fully and widely as possible. Thought needs to be preserved; books are vital elements of that preservation. Our society puts a premium less on knowledge for its own sake than the sales value of that knowledge. Therefore elements of information, particularly when its availability would be paid for by few, either remain unknown or never reach the book page. We — writers and potential readers — are the poorer for it.

The TCE process does not attempt to change the social norm but rather to expand the way that information can be made available and, yes, profitable, so it will be published in book form to far more people by many more writers. It simply makes books possible for more readers and for smaller readerships. That delights me immensely.

America — the world — is full of bright, articulate, insightful people who either have something to share or could have if they just knew that there is an easy-to-follow, self-directed path by which their words can reach readers — and for which they could be, at the same time, rewarded for having dared and worked to put them on paper.

Do I think that a real difference can be made by encouraging even more books in a world where too many books already go unread? You bet. Every new book writer is different and better for the act. And, yes, some of those books will contain bucketsful of trash. Many will follow well-trod paths, cliches ablazing. But one or a dozen might change the world in a way never thought possible before its words were read. That book, or that dozen, might never have existed had a process like TCE not been suggested. So that too delights and motivates me.

Finally, an introduction is an opportunity to thank others who have made this book, and its thoughts, possible, though they aren't responsible for its contents or any errors or folly it may contain.

My first guide to self-publishing was Dan Poynter's *The Self-Publishing Manual*, and from that came a valued personal friendship and much help. Jim Comiskey has been a steady prod to better work and clearer thought, while the Marci Manderscheids, Jim Becks, Jan Wahls, Dick Hennings, and Susan Gordons, plus a dozen other unsung enablers in the grove of extended education, kept my debtors away and let me share this information through seminars while I pruned it for print. Finally, my gratitude to the many chapters of the National Speakers Association who heard these words, mercifully condensed, and made the kind comments that both keep a new idea afloat and convinced its aging skipper that it should be shared even more widely.

Actually, I'd have published this book even if nobody liked it because I think it offers a perspective and process that's needed, is perfectly in tune with today's technological state, and rewards the doer — the writer, producer, promoter, and seller called collectively the self-publisher — with the money, prestige, and promise he or she deserves.

But I have delayed you too long from seeing what TCE means and how it works if you do. So end the introduction, start the book!

1 THE PREMISE

The premise is straightforward: "If you know something that others will pay to know, they will pay to know it many ways and by many means."

Of course premises are open to debate. But rather than debate, let's put our energy to more lucrative action. The purpose of these pages is to show you how, and why, to self-publish to tightly-targeted markets. If you are clever enough to do that, this book will also help you find areas of knowledge sufficiently compelling to make the premise come true.

The premise is straightforward: "If you know something that others will pay to know, they will pay to know it many ways and by many means."

In other words, if you wish to share information (which is what books do) and you want to be well-rewarded (in spendable tender, lots of it), that something you know that others will pay to know can make your wish come true.

For example, if you are the expert on widget burnishing but the process defies written explanation and your entire worldwide audience consists of seven scattered aficionados somewhere on the planet Earth, this book isn't for you.

But if you can tell others, say, how to sell widgets, there are many thousands eager to increase (better, double) their widget-selling commissions and they are accessible, you're already on the path to profitable publishing. And if you can expand the selling information and it would interest other widget hawkers to learn more by other means (such as articles, audio cassettes, videos, newsletters, or consulting), get reading!

Why am I talking about those other things — articles, tapes, newsletters, consulting — when what you really want to do is publish a book? Because what you are selling is none of those. You are selling information packaged as expertise, and those are simply the ways that information is sold. If you can sell your information one way, you can usually sell it, with modifications, most of the other ways.

I will focus on one of those ways here: a book. But if I totally isolated the book from the other means, a couple of things would happen. I would give you an incomplete, diluted view of the dynamics of information sharing akin to describing how to play baseball by focussing solely on bunting and running. And I'd be grossly derelict in showing you how, with only a fraction of additional effort, you could easily double your effectiveness and income.

Thus you will read about other means as well on these pages. Still, the overwhelming thrust of this text and its purpose is book-related, and with the exception of Chapter Seven, "Meeting That Need Through Other Information Dissemination Means," and half of the third section, EXPANDING, books and self-publishing to tightly-targeted markets are the core and substance of these pages. By understanding the book publication process you will be able to follow parallel steps for the other means, if they are applicable and you are interested.

Two more thoughts about the premise.

One, it's not enough just to have knowledge stored in your head. Even consultants have to share and adapt what they know for it to be profitable. They must convert what they know into applicable information upon which they or others can act.

The same for you. What makes information valuable to others is more than its existence. It must be available, understandable, and usable. How is that best done? By a means of information dissemination. Like a book.

The second point: you needn't be the foremost expert in the world to share information. In fact, you don't have to know much about your topic at all when you begin. The critical point is that the information you finally share is accurate, complete, and applicable. Not whether you spent a lifetime gathering it or a couple of no-nonsense months. The quality of your information will be judged by those who buy it. If it's good, they will want more of that good thing in other ways. If it's not, you've wasted a lot of time, money, and energy violating the premise. You simply don't know something that others will pay to know.

So far we've flirted with theory and fiddled with philosophy. Let's get to your book. Like, why not let some big-bucks publisher take it off your hands, send you fat royalty checks, and forget all this foolishness about doing it yourself? Stay tuned.

2 PUBLISHING AS USUAL: THE STANDARD PUBLISHER

There are two ways to publish a book, with some deviations. The conventional approach is to let a standard publisher do it for you. You write and they produce, promote, and — you hope — sell.

The second way is to do it yourself. You're in charge. You do it alone or, when necessary, hire others to do what they do better, quicker, or more economically, like a general contractor building a house. Except that here there is more than preparation and production. You must also promote your book, then sell it.

Most new writers are at best dimly aware of self-publishing. Others, aware, prefer to avoid or ignore it.

That's fine if you're writing a novel or an encyclopedia. But if you're planning to write a book for a tightly-targeted market, you cannot afford the luxury of such avoidance or the folly of such ignorance.

This chapter shows what standard publishers do. The next chapter discusses self-publishing. You must know the standard approach to understand how and why self-publishing is clearly better when writing to specifically identifiable clientele.

The Standard Approach

While there are thousands of published book writers and surely hundreds of ways of progressing from a concept to the bookstore shelf to the remainder pile, many follow a process similar to this:

1) The writer first finds a subject to write about, then researches to see (a) if another book currently exists, or soon will, about that subject; (b) if there is a market eager to buy the book; (c) which publishers produce books about that subject, and (d) which of those publishers should be approached in what order to produce the book.

(2) The writer prepares and submits a book proposal to the preferred publisher (or several) consisting of a query letter, an outline

or table of contents, a synopsis (if necessary), a reference/resource sheet, and (sometimes) a sample chapter or two.

(3) The publisher often sends the proposal and attachments to one or several advisors knowledgeable about the subject, and replies to the writer after receiving responses from the advisors.

(4) The publisher tells the writer yes, no, or perhaps (indicating what changes would be necessary for acceptance). If the publisher wishes to see more of the book before giving a firm reply, the writer will usually be asked to submit sample chapters (often three).

(5) If the chapters are acceptable, the publisher will offer a contract which will include a submission and payment schedule.

(6) Before offering the contract the publisher will conduct a marketing test, which may range from "asking around" to a full study.

(7) The writer researches and writes the book, then submits a draft.

(8) That manuscript is reviewed, edited, and returned to the writer for additions, alterations, and corrections.

(9) The writer submits a corrected draft.

(10) The book is prepared and printed. The publication date is often as much as 18 months after the corrected final draft is submitted.

(11) Often the writer promotes the book, on radio or TV or by other means, after the book is offered for sale.

Presuming that the writer finds a publisher who is interested in the book, what kind of payment (and when) might that writer expect for a nonfiction trade book bought by a standard house today?

Typical nonfiction book contract payment rates/dates

(1) Average advance against royalties, first-time nonfiction book: $5,000.

(2) Royalty schedule: cloth, 10% of list, first 4,999 copies; 12.5%, 5,000-9,999 copies; 15% = 10,000+; paperback, 6.5% of list, all copies.

(3) No royalty on books given for reviews, promotions, etc.

(4) The advance against royalties paid in three installments: (a) 1/3 after the contract is accepted and returned, (b) 1/3 after the final corrected draft is received, (c) 1/3 after the book is released for sale.

(5) Royalty payment paid every four (or six) months after the advance against royalties has been met.

(6) Against potential returns, 15% of the royalties due are held until the following payment period.

That's about as good as it gets. Some publishers have higher paying plateaus, such as 10% to 15,000 copies sold, 12.5% to 50,000, and 15% from 50,001. Some stop royalties at 10% or 12.5% whatever the quantity sold. Some start the cloth payment at 8%. Many withhold more than 15% for returns each pay period. A few pay every three months; some pay annually. Almost all pay for the period ending three months prior to the actual payment date. (For example, the royalties received on June 1 were for sales up to March 1.) Some fudge on the accounting of the actual number of books sold. And a large percentage don't pay on list (or retail) at all, rather on net (which means about a 50% reduction in what the writer receives if the royalty percentages are the same).

Is it lucrative to publish a book through a major publisher?

It can be.

It can also be a foolish investment of time, energy, and creative skills, if profit is the criterion.

Let's say, arbitrarily, that it takes you 12 hours a week extra time, for six months, to write, type, and initially edit your new book. That would be 288 hours (12 x 4 x 6) to get your book ready for print.

Further, let's say that a publisher accepts your book and prints 10,000 hardcover copies, to sell at $14.95. Following the standard royalty schedule, you would be paid 10% of list for the first 5,000, then 12.5% for the remaining 5,000. Calculating the book's price at $15, you would earn a total of $16,875 in royalties.

If you divide $16,875 by 288 hours you would be paid $59 an hour. Which, on the surface, isn't too bad. Particularly if you spend similar hours writing book after book— or the other hours earning a living.

Alas, you don't receive that $16,875 all at once— or very quickly.

If the publisher gave you an advance against royalties of $5,000, that would likely have been paid in this way:

(1) $1,666 when the contract was signed, after having written several chapters— perhaps three months after the query go-ahead;

(2) $1,666 when the final corrected draft was submitted— perhaps eight months after the query go-ahead, and

(3) $1,668 when the book was released for sale — perhaps 18-24 months after the publisher first responded affirmatively to your query.

One of the greatest shocks to new book writers is how long it takes to actually receive their money from a published book. The graph on the next page shows when that $16,875 might be received.

Remember, our example is for 10,000 cloth books at $14.95 (rounded off here to $15) with a $5,000 advance.

If it took eleven months to write the final draft from the time you received a go-ahead to your query, and another seven months for your book to see daylight, your book would first be offered for sale in the eighteenth month. Say that the publisher pays every six months and our chart starts with the first pay date, at the twenty-fourth month. And let's use a steadily declining rate of sales for simplicity, with 3,000 sold in the first six-month period.

That means that while your book was being written you receive $1,667, plus another $1,667 when the final corrected draft was submitted — a total of $3,332 the first year. In the second year you receive only the third part of the advance — $1,668 — as the book was released. Or a total of $5,000 in two years.

Since the advance is just that, 10% of the first $50,000 earned (or 3,333 books sold in our case), you wouldn't receive additional money at the first pay schedule because only 3,000 copies were sold. Post-royalty money would begin after the next 333 were bought. Thus at the thirtieth month you begin to receive royalties beyond the advance, or an additional $2,846.87.

The third year is the most lucrative: $6,625, with income in the subsequent three years $3,768.75, $1,237.50, and $243.75.

What is obvious is that publishing this way is less of a livelihood than a sinecure, an income booster to augment another, more substantial source of income. So much for the yacht and hobnobbing with the literati.

Is there any way to get rich through the major houses? Sure, as many have. One way is to write material so good, so riveting, so widely sought, that despite the happenchance promotion (or, oddly, because of it) your name and words catch buyers' fancy.

That means writing novels that do better than what the best are already doing, or something different, good, and liked. Or nonfiction books that hit the public appetite or need or curiosity at the right moment. The other way is to churn out more books, counting on volume to fill your coffers and create a cadre of readers eager for your next book. All of which means more sales,

Months after query go-ahead	24	30	36	42	48	54	60	66	72
Books sold	3000	2500	2000	1200	600	400	200	100	0
Royalty %	10	2000/10 500/12.5	12.5	12.5	12.5	12.5	12.5	12.5	12.5
Royalty earned	$4500	$3937.50	$3750	$2250	$1125	$750	$375	$187.50	0
15% withheld for returns	$675	$590.63	$562.50	$337.50	$168.75	$112.50	$56.25	$28.13	0
Paid	$3825 paid as advance	$2846.87; $1175 paid as advance	$3778.13	$2475	$1293.75	$806.25	$431.25	$215.62	$28.13

16 Self-Publishing to

the perception of you as a moneymaker by your publisher, a fatter advance, and better promotion.

There are actually eight areas where you might increase or accelerate your profits with a nonfiction book: topic, market, quicker book preparation, quality, royalty payment, marketing, quicker book production, and follow-up.

Find a topic that's particularly "hot" or needed and you should sell more books, increasing your profits. Select a market looking for or needing a particular book and the same should occur. And prepare books as quickly as possible to increase your total income from all of your books in publication.

But the others won't help you much. Unless it is poor, book quality is marginal to your profit stance, and is in the publisher's control anyway. You might shop for a better royalty schedule, but the field of differences is narrow. Publishers handle their own marketing and book production, so you can't change your own fate much there. And there is no follow-up by other means by most publishers. They sell your book and that's that. If you want to do anything more with that knowledge, good luck!

Will it sell?

Standard publishers have one overriding concern that writers cannot forget: to turn a profit and return a dividend to their stockholders. So their books, collectively, must make money. "Will it sell?" is the first and last question those truly in command must ask of each book. If it won't, you can bet your shoes it will be rejected or changed.

Sales are the fruit and promotion the fertilizer of publishing's true money trees. How those are done is where the TCE process and major publishers differ the most.

Major publishing houses aim their book sales at every literate American, plus any foreign rights they might grab along the way. So they can't fine tune topics too closely or they will eliminate huge chunks of potential buyers. They seek big topics. Broad subjects. Generic solutions that almost anybody can apply to his or her problems.

Which books thrive best with such a broad launching? Those that appeal to the greatest number of readers and those that appeal to the basest or most common interests. General books with wide readership.

Their marketing must be done on an equally grand scale, usually through bookstores, to have the books available for purchase when the promotion stimulates the buyer's urge. Libraries must also be convinced of widespread reader interest so the book will be bought for their collections. As must textbook buyers for use in classrooms nationwide.

That process is appropriate for mass selling of books. Novels of mayhem, murder, or madness, for example, may appeal to a wide spectrum of readers, particularly if they touch all three. A generic *How To Lose Weight* or *How To Reduce Your Income Taxes by 50%* will find favor in many households.

But how does the major publisher market *Secretaries: How To Lose Weight* or *Dentists: How To Reduce Your Malpractice Insurance Premiums by 50%*? Given a choice between generic books and the more limited markets, major houses pick generic books every time, despite the fact that there were 4,023,000 secretaries and 136,000 practicing dentists in the United States in 1986, and there are even more today.

Let's pursue the book for dentists and malpractice insurance for a moment. Presume that you know how to reduce malpractice insurance, are certain that every dentist would be interested, and you think that a book would be the best way to share this information widely and quickly.

You're in for a huge surprise if you think that a standard book publisher will accept that book! Their disinterest would have little to do with the worth of the idea, your credentials, or how well you write. You won't get a nibble for one very basic reason: the market is too small for the bigger houses to work.

Specific targets require marketing they don't do. The larger houses, with very few exceptions, produce books to be sold through distributors to bookstores, chains, schools, libraries, and other mass volume outlets. And dentists, other than by chance, do not buy books related to dentistry in mall bookstores or at the supermart. They buy them by mail, through association journals and newsletters, from display ads in dental-related magazines, at conventions, through reviews in their publications, and by word-of-mouth. So almost all standard publishers will reject your query since they didn't get big by producing books that sell small.

Yet some do work specialty markets, and your book may be just what they are seeking. Beware. An example from a student I recently taught shows why. He proposed a book about word processing to a major publisher selling by direct mail to the business world (as well as through bookstores). They were interested and suggested a 700-page how-to text in workbook form that they would sell for $80. He would receive an advance of $4,000-6,000 against royalties of 5% of the list price, or $4 for every $80 item sold. Which means, if his advance was $5,000, he wouldn't get another cent until the publisher had made $100,000. And for the author to earn $50,000 in profit the publisher must reap $1,000,000!

The TCE process that this book outlines would have you earn at least half of that million dollars as profit — or ten times, at least, what you would earn from a standard publisher generous enough even to be interested in selling your information!

So standard publishers aren't the way to sell information to tightly-targeted markets.

The final insult...

Even if a standard publisher accepted your book and brought it to print they will probably abandon it if it doesn't sell well and quickly. At the risk of generalizing to make a point, promotion at many of the larger publishing houses follows the "flaming arrow" approach. The house launches 20 or 100 books at once, shooting all of their arrows skyward. They have told the public in advance to watch for certain books, those bearing the names of their popular authors, their proven moneymakers. The publisher watches the rest, and if one or another of the new arrows catches fire when it lands, it gets fanned. That is, the publisher blows up instant promotion and prints more copies to meet the demand, which is increased by the new promotion. After working them for obvious sales and trying to earn back at least production costs and the paid advance, the rest are left to die quietly.

There's nothing evil or particularly absurd about the way standard publishers run their business given their large-scale orientation, size, and relative isolation from the book buyer. But there's nothing to commend it for a book to a tightly-targeted market either.

There's simply a better way

If you're eager to share specific information with an identified, tightly-targeted market, and, yes, you too would like to earn a handsome profit like the standard publishers, and, moreover, you'd like much more of it and sooner, publishing houses are the wrong avenue for your book.

That the major houses opt for broad markets is a huge blessing for you. It's an entrepreneur's dream! From either the book to secretaries or dentists — which are but two examples from thousands of other ideas and titles — you could earn 50% profit or more from each book (not 6-15%), then double that again by other means, at the same time creating an empire of lifetime earnings.

Even if major publishers were interested in limited market books, publishing through them would at best reward you with small royalties, slow payments, and their generally fitful marketing practices. And they would do nothing to promote the follow-up or to enhance your empire. Which is where the TCE process functions best.

With TCE you start with a market, figure out what it needs, write a book that meets that need, produce the book yourself (contracting out what others do better), sell directly to your chosen market, expand the ways you share that information by either other information means or more books, and use all of the knowledge gained and products developed to create an on-going empire.

In the next chapter we will see how self-publishing the TCE way does far better what standard publishers don't do well at all: getting your tightly-targeted book to all of your market quickly and very profitably.

3 AN ALTERNATIVE: A SELF-PUBLISHED BOOK TO TIGHTLY-TARGETED MARKETS

We said at the beginning of the last chapter that there are two ways to publish a book: through a standard publisher or by doing it yourself.

That's not quite true. There are really three key ways to get a book published, and you do two of them yourself. They differ by how the book will be marketed and, to a lesser degree, by the organizational steps leading up to that marketing.

We've discussed the first method, standard publishing, at least sufficiently to see that it isn't the preferred path for tightly-targeted books.

The second method draws from both camps. It is self-publishing with standard marketing. Which means that the self-publisher produces the book but then tries to sell it by using standard publishing methods.

The third method is self-publishing the TCE way.

The second and third methods share the same self-publishing developmental stages of preparation, production, and promotion. They are virtually identical at the production stage, and thus the two best how-to books about self-publishing, the *Self-Publishing Manual* and Tom and Marilyn Ross's *The Complete Guide to Self-Publishing*, are excellent guides concerning a book's production and much of its preparation.

The biggest difference lies in promotion.

The marketing thrust of the Poynter and Ross books envisions a successful self-publisher as a person who produces his or her own book and markets it well and widely by using the same basic selling techniques as larger, standard publishers, though with more persistence and some modification. They allow for additional creativity and tailoring to a specific market but see that as secondary. Most sales would come through bookstores, distributors, libraries, and chains; good reviews would draw additional sales. Selling to tightly-targeted markets is poorly addressed, as is direct marketing by mail.

The TCE process — which, again, stands for targeted, customized, and expanded — requires a much different approach to marketing for the simple reason that the book won't be bought at bookstores or chains. Rather, it is written specifically — customized — to a clearly defined market and is sold directly to the people in that market, primarily by mail, secondarily by more general techniques such as reviews in appropriate journals or newsletters, display ads in those same vehicles, catalogs or card decks directed to that market, a booth at regional meetings or the convention, articles that market folk would read, and other means mentioned by Poynter or Ross, and also explained in John Kremer's *1001 Ways To Market Your Book.*

The order of activity and planning is different too. The reader isn't a vague half-form dimly floating in space to whom the book is generally written. In the TCE process the reader is a buyer from a clearly-defined and understood market, a person who will purchase the book for a very precise reason and who expects its contents to do very specific things. So the definition of that reader/buyer and what he or she will (or will not) buy precede the writing. In fact, before a word of text goes on paper the writer knows the selling plugs in the advertisement or sales cover letter that will make the buyer rush to order the book!

There's more. Where standard publishers stop at book production and self-publishing texts hint at topic life after print, the "E" of the TCE process stands for "expanded," or the greater use of the information being sold on the book page.

Where the TCE process differs is by integrating this expansion by other information dissemination means early into the process. It identifies all of the ways by which that information can be sold, designs a developmental path, and uses the book's preparation as a source and spur to create other means before, during, and after the book appears in final form. It also helps structure the book so that it can serve as a valuable on-going information source for other means. One example would be the creation and implementation of a seminar for which the book is a vital workbook and take-home tool.

In standard and conventional self-publishing money flows as long as the book is bought, and when that last copy goes income stops. Not so the TCE way.

Why should you self-publish the TCE way?

Because you can get your words in print, earn far more money, greatly reduce the time it takes to put those words in published book form, control the contents and appearance of your book, direct the ways by which your information and book are sold, and integrate into and around your book the other means by which that same, similar, or subsequent information can also be sold.

Some specifics, in contrast to following the standard publishing model already discussed:

(1) You needn't convince any other publishers that your ideas and words are worth their time, energy, and investment. That can save you months or years of time.

(2) You can set your own pace for the book's preparation, production, and promotion.

(3) Your profit per book may well exceed 60-65%, and should top 50% of net. It can be yours the moment payment is received, without reserve for returns.

(4) You can determine how many books to print, when, and how they will be bound or customized for market needs.

(5) You won't be abandoned by a publisher if your book doesn't sell quickly and well — unless you give up on yourself! You are in control of promotion and sales, from inception to remaindering.

What's the catch?

Writing a book is hard, exacting work. Publishing it is three times harder, and continues until the last copy is bought, burned, or donated. If you earn five or ten times as much by self-publishing, you earn every cent. That's risk money because it's your capital that pays for preparation, production, and promotion. Every trip to the library, every illustration or board or shipping invoice or flyer comes from your coffers — most of it long before a dime returns.

What hurts most is the disdain in which you will be held for having invested dearly in putting your ideas and words in print, for self-publishing to others both in the trade and outside it is held in low esteem. Generally the unknowing assume that you couldn't get a standard publisher to accept your book so you had to do it yourself! (Which, incidentally, may be true but speaks as much to the weakness of standard publishers as to your ideas and writing abilities.)

It's labyrinthian and perilous too. Plenty of steps to follow, one thing after another, pitfalls, nobody to pull you through and shout praises or point before you step off some financial cliff...

Well, who promised you it would be fun? (But it is, usually.) Who guaranteed you utter and certain success? (That can happen nevertheless.)

And anyway, what worth doing doesn't have a learning curve and pitfalls and financial cliffs and the great, singular satisfaction of seeing the results helping others build a better world?

Life's a game, and so is self-publishing. As serious a game as you want to make it. The prize can be a pot of gold and your words in print for all time. Want to play? Our game is called TCE and it requires 14 steps. Step one is next!

TARGETING

4 FINDING, DEFINING, AND QUALIFYING THE TARGET MARKET

"Targeted" means knowing specifically who will buy your book, why, how much they will pay (and won't), how they would hear about your book, and what your promotion must say to get them to make that purchase.

In other words, you don't write a word until you've answered those questions. Then every word you do write is written directly to that market and fulfills each and every promise made in the promotion. If you are writing a book telling bank tellers how to become bank presidents, the book will outline, then detail, precisely how that rise can be made and how the reader can follow the advice. Your book will be written to ambitious bank tellers, period. To, it seems, millions of them.

So you must first pick a group of people to write to.

That group of people is your market. Tightly-targeted books are written to specific people, to clearly identifiable "somebodies." The first step is finding the right target, then defining and qualifying it.

Writing to "anybody" won't do if you plan to self-publish, have limitations on your budget, and hope to receive a bountiful profit soon. Save the broad markets for standard publishers who have the money and, sometimes, the moxie to make them work.

Rather, think small and tight. Pick a target for your book that is definable and accessible, and has a need that it wants to meet plus the funds and desire to buy a book to do so. If that's not enough, there must also be a sufficient number of those somebodies eager and able to buy your book.

Many thousands of just such markets exist. There is a shockingly large number of somebodies joined together by like interests and needs who will buy a book to meet them. Best yet, they aren't very hard to find.

Let's amplify and restate the qualifications for a TCE target market, to better serve as a guide. To be an acceptable TCE market a group of people must:

(1) **share something in common**, such as a profession (doctors, placement directors, welders), job title (fulfillment packers, food vendors, janitors), or experience (Korean War veterans, former Chicago Cubs);

(2) **appear on** an accessible, affordable, and current or "cleaned" **mailing list;**

(3) **share a pressing need** or needs;

(4) **have** both a sufficient desire and the **income to seek and afford information** about meeting that need, and

(5) **be sufficiently numerous** to make provision of the information profitable to the provider.

All five are important, and each must be interpreted in terms of the best interests of publishing your book. In (1), for example, not all who share a common interest will qualify. If the interest they share is their fierce individualism, that would likely preclude each from buying a book that others bought, at least for that reason. If what binds them together is a hatred of books, the group is even less promising for your purposes.

The second qualification comes from the need to make the targeted market aware of the book's existence and desirability. You simply must know who and where the buyers are. By extension, since that market is likely to be scattered, they will most likely be contacted promotionally by mail. Therefore a current mailing list is doubly important. Which excludes people without reasonably fixed addresses, like transients or the homeless, as good markets for TCE books, though they indeed share something vital in common and have a pressing need.

Income is also a factor, as noted in qualification four. The need your book meets must, in the minds of the market, be worth the cost of that book. And the buyers must have sufficient capital to make that purchase. However worthy the advice or information, it will not be bought by the utterly destitute.

And there simply must be enough people in the market able and eager to buy your book to make its preparation and production worthwhile.

To speak in more specific terms for the remainder of this text, let's say that you plan to earn $50,000 profit from your first tightly-targeted, self-published book. Plus you plan to earn that much again by other means. Which doesn't limit you to $50,000 from either source, or $100,000 in total, but simply gives us firm numbers to work with on these pages.

How many people must there be in your target market to earn that $50,000 book profit? Say that it costs you $4,000 to produce the book. Your market would need only 18 people — if every one of them bought a copy and paid $3,000 for it!

Alas, most markets don't buy at a 100% ratio nor will they pay $3,000 a copy. In fact, most buyers start hedging when a book costs about $12, think very long at $25, and are in full retreat at $50 — significantly short of $3,000. Since promotional costs rise in close ratio to the number in the market to be contacted, a profit of $50,000 is far more likely to require a market that numbers from 30,000 to 75,000.

Let's add some more variables to your $50,000 book profit goal, to establish a base that we can use for calculations for the rest of this book. Let's say that (1) you are offering the only book that meets the need, (2) your book will cost $15 (though you will actually sell it for $14.95 because a buyer will mentally justify spending "$14 and change" more easily than $15), (3) you will sell the book directly to the buyer, eliminating any handlers' discounts, (4) the buyer will pay the postage and tax as part of the purchase price add-on, (5) it will cost you 50% of the selling price to produce, promote, and market your book, and (6) you will sell the book to 10% of your targeted market. Given those conditions, to reap a $50,000 profit your targeted market must have 66,667 buyers.

How could you reduce that number? You could cut it in half by doubling the book price — or by selling to 20% instead of 10% of your targeted market. If you did both you would need a target market of only 16,667! Another obvious way would be to reduce production, promotion, and marketing costs, which are very high at 50%. But the very best way to hit the optimum profit level is to strike right at the heart of the market's greatest need(s) and make your book irresistible in every way.

Let me pose an additional thought now, the value of which will become more evident as this book progresses. Many markets will meet all five qualifications, yet among them some markets will yield one book and little else while others will produce enough riches to last a lifetime. Three characteristics are found in the latter: continual growth of the market, a quick turnover of its members, and/or a steady development of new needs.

Must you be a member of a group or market to write about it?

No, but the process will probably be quicker and more certain if you do share at least some of the same interests.

Why? Because you will have a better, more intimate sense of the group's problems and needs, you will have a better understanding of its buying practices and preferences, you may have access to the group's leaders or others more knowledgeable about the topic of your book, and you may have preferred access to the group's newsletter, mailing list, convention or meeting plans, and other "inside" information.

That you are not a member can be partially offset by careful research, joining the group and getting quickly integrated into its activities, co-authoring with a member or a person well-informed of its activities, and/or having a member or well-informed person accessible with whom you can frequently verify the validity of your book's content.

How can you check on the existence and size of accessible markets?

Since a mailing list is essential and its size is a key determinant to market appropriateness, perhaps the best source would be directories or catalogs of mailing lists. Available in most libraries is a quarterly publication called *Direct Mail Lists Rate and Data* published by Standard Rate and Data Services. A current SRDS directory contains thousands of lists available to you through both the list providers and brokers, their rental or purchase cost, forms in which the list can be provided (Cheshire labels, press-on labels, and magnetic tapes are the most common), ways a list can be sub-divided, how long it takes for the list to be sent, restrictions on its use, and other information. As important here, the directory tells the number of names currently listed, by total and sometimes by area or category.

Many list providers also make their catalogs available, so a call or letter to those companies serving your target field will yield similar information to that found in the SRDS directories, usually with more details. For example, using such a catalog from American Business Lists, Inc. from January, 1988, a random selection of those lists of more than 30,000 names includes:

What kinds of groups/professions have 30,000+ listed?

A sample list on the next page gives an idea of the kinds of markets available for a TCE book. These names, selected from the *Yellow Pages*, are sold by American Business Lists, Inc., P.O. Box 27347, Omaha, NE 68127.

Public accountants	118,154
Air conditioning contractors/systems	46,533
Aircraft owners	293,728
Aircraft pilots	648,101
Alteration contractors	49,508
Antiques, dealers in	30,381
Architects	37,264
Associations	37,901
Attorneys	414,596
Auto Body, Repairing and Painting	67,855
Auto Dealers, Used Car	71,774
Auto Parts & Supplies, Retail/New	61,112
Auto Repair & Service	181,520
Banks	52,448
Barbers	65,613
Bars/Lounges	53,291
Beauty Salons	206,685
Beer Parlors	53,291
Brake Services	32,653
Building Contractors	67,640
Carpet & Rug Dealers, New	34,868
Caterers	38,532
Child Care Services	37,205
Chiropractors	43,308
Churches	225,261
Cleaners, Service	46,001
Clergy	63,229
Clinics	34,036
Clubs, Private	30,074
Contractors, Building	67,640
Contractors, Excavating	31,526
Contractors, General	114,885
Contractors, Heating & Ventilating	43,439
Contractors, Remodeling & Repairing	49,508
Day Nurseries & Child Care	37,205
Decorators	30,241
Dentists	151,797
Drive-In Restaurants	309,770
Druggists, Retail	55,468
Electric Contractors	52,366
Florists, Retail	46,789
Foods, Carry Out	39,099
Furniture Dealers, Retail	40,394
Gasoline Service Stations	120,896
Gift Shops	67,372
Government Offices, City, Village, Township	42,991
Government Offices, U.S.	39,231
Grocers, Retail	145,705
Hardware, Retail	34,970
Hotels and Motels	73,068
Insurance Agencies	191,898
Jewelers, Retail	41,436
Liquors, On-Sale Retail	53,291
Liquors, Retail	40,534
Loans	51,512
Machine Shops	35,790
Marriage & Family Counselors	39,568
Mortgages	46,179
Optometrists	31,767
Paint, Retail	34,698
Physicians & Surgeons	362,294
Pizza Parlors	47,265
Plumbing Contractors	51,358
Printers	55,177
Real Estate Agencies	170,669
Real Estate Agents	357,660
Restaurants	309,770
Roofing Contractors	31,585
Schools	91,669
Shoes, Retail	40,006
Social Service Organizations	45,976
Stock Broker Executives	30,061
Tax Reporting Services	40,990
Tire Dealers, Retail	42,352
Towing, Automotive	40,437
Travel Agencies & Bureaus	34,242
Truckers	212,720
Veterinarians	43,492
Women's Apparel, Retail	63,895

If your targeted field includes associations, check the *Encyclopedia of Associations* available at most libraries. It can help in two ways: the current membership and the names of the publications the association produces. Often you may rent both the membership list and the publication subscriber list, though sometimes these are for members only. It would make little sense to rent both if the magazine is distributed exclusively to members. The best situation for you is when the publication accepts outside subscriptions, is widely bought by those in the field, is sent to all members, lists every recipient, and that list can be rented by the public.

SRDS also publishes three monthlies called *Newspaper Rates and Data, Business Publications Rate and Data,* and *Consumer Magazines and Agri-Media Rates and Data* which list other publications, with circulation statistics, which those in the targeted field might read in a library. A quick cross-check with the SRDS mailing list directory or a letter or call to the publication itself will reveal whether the subscription list is rentable.

Often the fastest way to identify those most interested in a topic is to find the most highly respected newsletter in the field. How do you test respect? Probably by asking those in the target field receiving all available publications. To find addresses and pertinent information about the many newsletters now available, see the *Newsletters Directory,* formerly called the *National Directory of Newsletters.*

And don't forget an obvious source of general data: the many almanacs in your library, such as the *The World Almanac and Book of Facts.*

The purpose of this step? To find, define, and qualify your book's target market. You have to write to a specific collective somebody — the right somebody. In the following chapter we will further qualify that market by its need.

But before that, your task will be easier if you see an example being developed as we go along, one that we can follow step-by-step so that you can see ways to apply the information and suggestions directly to your own book.

EXAMPLE

My task when structuring this book was to find an example that would serve as a model for every reader, plus one that was broad enough to provide information or guidance at every step.

Two paths quickly suggested themselves. I could use an example with a business orientation, which might result in books with titles like *How To Join America's Most Prosperous Shoe Retailers* or *Stock Brokers: Stop Killing Yourself and Start Earning Real Top Dollar*. I'd play on a powerful motivation to buy and read a book: bald greed.

But that path was too easy. The problem was that many potential book publishers have tightly-targeted markets in areas where motivations are less obvious but no less valid or valuable.

So I turned to the second path, focussing on a professional position where greed cannot be so openly addressed and where vocational promotion is not a factor, thinking that any book that would meet our TCE criteria and showed sufficient promise of profit in this second category would easily do so, with modest adaptation, in the first. I chose school principals as the target market.

Mind you, I had no idea whether principals would satisfy the five qualifying requirements nor whether our desire to earn $50,000 profit from a book for them, and double it later, would be possible. Nor did I know much about their needs, what makes them tick, or whether they would buy a book about themselves and their vocation, or something somehow linked to it. Mostly what I knew about school principals came from my own youth when I was certain that knowing nothing about them was too much. And that they all wore glasses. What I discovered as an adult intent upon knowing whether they would contribute to my wealth you will read on these pages.

(On the other hand, I am paying to print every word in this book. If they had failed badly you wouldn't be reading about them at all, but some other professional group which didn't fail. As it is, principals get a solid A- as a source for the first $50,000 in profits but, at best, a D+ for the next $50,000. Good enough to show you how to make your market an even better choice. What also intrigued me about principals were some exciting discoveries I made along the way that could keep me, or you, very profitably publishing in this field for a lifetime. I'll share those with you too.)

Do they meet the qualifying criteria?

Let's see.

(1) Do they "share something in common"? Yep, they are all principals, which wraps profession, job title, and experience into one. They mainly followed the same path to a key position in their pro-

fession, they have a lifetime dedication to education, and none of them is getting rich that way. Another set of commonly-shared factors is particularly important to book publishers: they are literate, book-oriented, likely to seek answers from written sources, and can buy school- or principal-related publications out of their school budgets.

(2) Do they appear on an accessible, affordable, and current or cleaned mailing list? Yep again. They are isolated on a half-dozen acceptable lists, but two in a 1988 SRDS directory seem the most appropriate because of their cost and breakdown.

(3) Presumably they share many pressing needs. More on that in the next chapter.

(4) Do they have have the desire and income to seek and afford my information? The desire is often provoked by the need, so let's discuss that with need later. We can say they share a common desire to improve their lot!

Can they afford it? A library can help a bit here. Some 200 jobs comprising 60% of those in the economy are generally described, with wages and trends, in the *Occupational Outlook Handbook*, Bulletin 2250, of the U.S. Department of Labor Statistics, usually found in the reference or government documents section. Though the statistics are usually three years out of date, they show in a rough way how much the practitioners earn. The listing called "Education Administrators" in the 1987-8 edition appears on pages 34-6.

How does that pay range of $36,452 to $42,094 for principals compare to the average income? A look at the current *World Almanac* is helpful. Comparable average income by various cities for that same year was:

Tampa, Florida	$ 15,674
Memphis, Tennessee	17,481
Dallas, Texas.	20,976
New York City, New York	23,111
San Jose, California	23,703

Thus the principals were earning about twice the average income then. It's highly likely that a benefit-laden book for $15 would fit in their budgets. Particularly if they can buy it with school funds. So a yes here too.

(5) The stopper in many cases is the fifth qualifier. "Are they sufficiently numerous to make provision of the information profitable to the provider?"

Tightly-Targeted Markets

Education Administrators

(D.O.T. 075.117-010, -018; 090.117 except -034, .167; 091.107; 092.137; 094.107, .117-010, -014; 094.167-010; 096.167-010, -014; 097.167; 099.117 except -022; 169.267-022; 239.137-010)

Nature of the Work

Smooth operation of an educational institution requires competent administrators. Education administrators provide direction, leadership, and day-to-day management of educational activities in preschools; elementary, secondary, religious, vocational, and technical schools; colleges and universities; businesses; correctional institutions; museums; and job training and community service organizations. They set educational standards and goals and set up policies and procedures to carry them out. Education administrators develop academic programs; hire, train, and motivate teachers and other staff; manage guidance and other services to students; administer recordkeeping; prepare budgets; handle relations with parents, prospective students, employers, or others outside of education; and perform numerous other activities.

They work through and supervise subordinate managers, management support staff, teachers, counselors, librarians, coaches, and others. In a small organization, such as a day care center, there may be one administrator who handles all functions. In a major university or large school system, responsiblities are divided among many administrators, organized in a hierarchy.

Principals manage elementary and secondary schools. They set the academic tone—high-quality instruction is their most important responsibility. Principals hire and assign teachers and other staff, help them improve their skills, and evaluate them. They confer with them—advising, explaining, or answering procedural questions. They visit classrooms, review instructional objectives, and examine learning materials. They also meet with other administrators, students, parents, and representatives of community organizations. They prepare budgets and reports, keep track of attendance, and see that supplies are requisitioned and allocated.

Assistant principals may perform principals' duties and usually handle discipline, social and recreational programs, health and safety, and building and grounds maintenance. They may also counsel students on personal, educational, or vocational matters.

Public schools are also managed by administrators in school district central offices. This group includes education supervisors, who direct subject area programs such as English, music, vocational education, special education, and mathematics. They plan, evaluate, and improve curriculum and teaching techniques and help teachers improve their skills and learn about new methods and materials. This group also includes directors of programs such as guidance, school psychology, athletics, curriculum development, and audiovisual materials.

In colleges and universities, academic deans, also known as deans of faculty, provosts, or university deans, assist presidents and develop budgets and academic policies and programs. They direct and coordinate activities of deans and chairpersons of individual colleges and academic departments.

College or university department heads or chairpersons are in charge of departments such as English, biological science, or mathematics. They coordinate schedules of classes and teaching assignments, propose budgets, recruit and interview applicants for teaching positions, and perform other administrative duties in addition to teaching.

Higher education administrators also provide student services. Deans of students, also known as vice-presidents of student affairs or directors of student services, direct and coordinate admissions, foreign student services, and health and counseling services, as well as social, recreation, and related programs. They set and enforce student personnel policies and administer discipline. In a small college, they may counsel students. Registrars are custodians of students' education records. They prepare student transcripts, evaluate academic records, and analyze registration statistics. Directors of admissions manage the process of admitting students, oversee the preparation of college catalogs, recruit students, and work closely with financial aid directors, who oversee scholarship, fellowship, and loan programs. Directors of student activities plan and arrange social, cultural, and recreational activities, assist student-run organizations and orient new students. Athletic directors plan and direct intramural and intercollegiate athletic activities, including publicity for athletic events, preparation of budgets, and supervision of coaches.

Working Conditions
Education administrators may work alone in offices but also meet with the staffs they supervise, other administrators, students, alumni, and others. Some jobs include travel.

Some education administrators work more than 40 hours a week, including some nights and weekends when school activities take place. Unlike teachers, they usually work year round.

Employment
Education administrators held about 288,000 jobs in 1986. More than 90 percent were in educational services—in elementary, secondary, and technical schools and colleges and universities. Some worked in child day care centers, religious organizations, job training centers, State departments of education, and businesses and other organizations that provide training activities for their employees.

Training, Other Qualifications, and Advancement
Education administrator is not usually an entry level job. Most education administrators begin their careers in other related occupations. Because of the diversity of duties and levels of responsibility, their educational backgrounds and experience vary considerably. Principals, assistant principals, central office administrators, and academic deans usually have taught or held another related job before moving into administration. Some teachers move directly into principalships; others first gain experience in a central office administrative job. In some cases, administrators move up from related staff jobs such as recruiter, residence hall director, or financial aid or admissions officer. To be considered for education administrator positions, workers must first prove themselves in their current jobs. In evaluating candidates, superiors look for determination, confidence, innovativeness, motivation, and managerial attributes such as ability to make sound decisions, to organize and coordinate work efficiently, and to establish good personal relationships with and motivate others. Knowledge of management principles and practices, gained through work experience and formal education, is important.

Principals and assistant principals in all 50 States and the District of Columbia need a master's degree or higher in education administration and a State teaching certificate. Many principals have a doctorate.

Academic deans usually have a doctorate in their specialty. Admissions, student affairs, and financial aid directors and registrars often start in related staff jobs with bachelor's degrees—any field is usually acceptable—and get advanced degrees in student counseling and personnel services or higher education administration. A Ph.D. or Ed.D. is usually necessary for top student personnel positions. Courses in data processing are an asset in admissions, records, and financial work.

Advanced degrees in education administration are offered in many colleges and universities. The National Council for Accreditation of Teacher Education accredits programs at over 250 campuses. There are 92 doctorate programs in higher education administration. Graduate programs in student counseling and personnel services are offered in about 500 colleges and universities. Education administration degree programs include courses in school management, school law, school finance and budgeting, curriculum development and evaluation, research design and data analysis, community relations, politics in education, and leadership.

Education administrators advance by moving up an administrative hierarchy or transferring to larger schools or systems. Some become administrators in industries outside education.

Tightly-Targeted Markets

Job Outlook

Employment of education administrators is expected to grow more slowly than the average for all occupations through the year 2000. Most job openings will be to replace administrators who leave the profession.

Demand for education administrators is determined primarily by enrollments. Elementary school enrollments are expected to increase moderately through the year 2000; secondary school enrollments are expected to increase only slightly. College enrollments should decline through the mid-1990's and then begin to increase, but will still be below the 1986 level in the year 2000. Therefore, jobs for elementary school administrators are likely to grow faster than for other school administrators.

The number of education administrators employed depends largely on State and local expenditures for education. Pressure from taxpayers to limit spending could result in fewer administrators than anticipated; pressures to increase spending to improve the quality of education could result in more.

Substantial competition is expected for jobs as principals, assistant principals, and central office administrators. Many teachers and other staff meet the education and experience requirements for these jobs and seek promotion. However, the number of openings is relatively small, so generally only the most highly qualified are selected.

Earnings

The median annual salary for education administrators who worked full time was $32,000 in 1986. The middle 50 percent earned between $23,000 and $41,000.

Salaries of education administrators vary according to position, level of responsibility and experience, and the size and location of the institution.

According to the Educational Research Service, Inc., average salaries for principals and assistant principals in the school year 1986-87 were as follows:

Principals:
Senior high school $47,896
Junior high/middle school........ 44,861
Elementary school............... 41,536

Assistant principals:
Senior high school 39,758
Junior high/middle school........ 37,958
Elementary school............... 34,347

In 1986-87, according to the College and University Personnel Association, median annual salaries for selected administrators in higher education were as follows:

Academic deans:
Medicine $120,000
Law.......................... 89,000
Engineering................... 68,496
Arts and sciences 57,681
Business...................... 55,790
Education 55,259
Social sciences................ 42,400
Mathematics 40,750
Student services directors:
Admissions and registrar........ 38,853
Development and alumni
affairs..................... 38,713
Student financial 30,899
Student activities.............. 27,214

Related Occupations

Education administrators apply organizational and leadership skills to provide services to individuals. Related occupations include health services administrators, social service agency administrators, recreation and park managers, museum directors, library directors, and professional and membership organization executives.

Using our guiding numbers of a $15 book and a 10% market sale, we would need 66,667 to earn our $50,000 profit from the book. The two most appropriate mailing lists gave these results:

Mailing Lists: School Principals

List #1, at $35/thousand:

Classification	Number	Sub-Total	Cost
Public Schools			
K-6	29,532		$ 1,033.62
K-8	12,966		454.86
K-12	1,013		35.46
7-8	5,663		198.21
7-12	7,442		260.47
10-12	3,427		119.94
		60,073	2,102.56
Catholic schools			
elementary	9,551		334.29
secondary	1,848		64.68
K-12	342		11.97
		11,741	410.94
Private schools			
elementary	2,111		73.88
secondary	767		26.85
K-12	767		26.85
		3,645	127.58
TOTALS		75,459	$ 2,641.08

List #2, at $25/thousand:

	Number	Cost
Elementary school principals	50,865	$ 1,271.63
Junior high school principals	12,535	313.37
Senior high school principals	15,591	389.77
TOTALS	78,991	$ 1,974.77

Tightly-Targeted Markets

So the totals of 75,459 or 78,991 are well in the comfort zone if the book were directed to principals in general. List one, itemized, also yields these sub-divisions:

Elementary school principals	55,203
Middle school principals	8,278
High school principals	4,536

What do the mailing list numbers suggest?

There are principals and there are principals. The tighter you focus the easier it is to find them and put a once-only book in their hands. (How many books are there for principals of Lutheran or Baptist grade 7-8 schools that dwell specifically on their problems?) But there's a point beyond which the cost of the book and the penetration percentage would have to be so high that profits would stop. What do the mailing list numbers tell us?

(1) The largest market would be for a book topic for all principals of all schools, regardless of level or public/private funding: 75-79,000.
(2) An acceptable market would be:
   (a) public school principals: 60,000
   (b) elementary school principals: 55,000
   (c) private life of principal, outside of school (excluding priests and nuns as likely buyers): 60-70,000
(3) Unacceptable TCE book markets as too small:
   (a) Catholic school principals
   (b) Private school principals
   (c) Middle school principals
   (d) High school principals
(4) If both lists are otherwise acceptable (and the specific breakdown of List 1 isn't necessary), List 2 is preferred for its lower price.

Another kind of list that simplifies sales

If you are going to sell your book person-to-person, you will primarily use direct mail. Yet most target markets bond together into associations, guilds, unions, fraternities, brotherhoods, sisterhoods, clubs, groups, and soon. These gatherings often have meetings, conventions, and newsletters. They make book selling far easier.

If we can locate such units for principals we have another mailing list, or many, and other ways to sell to our targeted market, such as a booth at the convention or through display or classified ads in the newsletter. Where do we look? In the current edition of the *Encyclopedia of Associations*.

What do we find in the 1988 edition for principals? (And what is also available for "superintendents and top school administrators," on the possibility that when we select a book topic there may be selling overlap to them?

Association of Principals, Superintendents, Top School Administrators

Principals

NASSP, National Association of Secondary School Principals; 37,000 members, begun in 1916, located in Reston, VA: annual convention (with exhibits)

NAESP, National Association of Elementary School Principals; 22,000, 1921, Alexandria, VA; annual convention (with exhibits)

NATTS, National Association of Trade and Technical Principals; 1,002, 1965, Washington, DC; annual convention (with exhibits)

National Conference of Yeshiva Principals; 1,000, 1947, New York City; meets twice a year

NAPSG, National Association of Principals of Schools for Girls; 500, 1920, Hendersonville, NC; annual conference

HA, Headmasters Association; 263, 1893, Simsbury, CT; annual meeting

CDSHA, County Day School Headmasters Association of the United States; 100, 1912, Norfolk, VA; annual meeting

Superintendents and Top School Administrators

AASA, American Association of School Administrators; 18,000, 1865, Arlington, VA; annual convention

AFSA, American Federation of School Administrators; 10,000, 1971, New York City; triennial meeting

NABSE, National Alliance of Black School Educators; 3,000, 1970, Washington, DC: annual convention (with exhibits)

CAESD, Conference of Educational Administrators Serving the Deaf; 355, 1868, Washington, DC; annual conference (with exhibits)

Source: *Encyclopedia of Associations*, 1988 edition

An intriguing surprise

A person seeking information with tunnel vision might well overlook some intriguing markets that would otherwise not be evident. For example, along with lists of principals in the SRDS directory was a tally of teachers by grade.

Wouldn't teachers of particular grades run to buy a book that focussed specifically on that year of the educational process? But could we find a comparable 66,667 people to buy a $15 book, or some balance of those numbers? Let's arbitrarily pick out fifth grade. There are 90,874 teachers at that level, plus a suspicion on my part that some fourth or sixth grade teachers might buy a copy too, as would principals and many elementary school education departments at colleges.

I scoured three major libraries well, with all of their listings of other key libraries, and could not find one book written specifically to fifth grade teachers. So I asked some fifth grade teachers and they knew of nothing other than the teachers' guidebooks for texts they used in class.

Which put my mind to wandering. If a mate or friend were to write a book for fifth grade teachers and I were to write one for principals, how easy it would be to sell two at once by mail. The single greatest expense, promotion, would be halved at one shot.

If I wrote a book for fifth grade teachers, I could use the format and hire a fleet of other writers (some, teachers) to do a book on each of the other elementary years built around that structure, which I could edit and publish as a series.

Why not write similar books for teachers of specific subjects, like art, music, physical education, or English as a Second Language? Those might also be done by year or, better, by year groups like grades 1-3 and 4-6.

Of course if I'm writing a book for fifth grade teachers, might I not write a book for parents of fifth grade students? The relationship must change rather dramatically each year at that formative level, and by focussing on the child's level of development, how the school deals with that, and how parents could best address it would seem to result in a book that many if not most parents would want to read. The market would be new every year and would ultimately include every parent in America. Imagine if they bought such a book for every year from kindergarten up!

Exciting, isn't it? Maybe we'll come back to this later.

5 FINDING AND DEFINING A SPECIFIC MARKET NEED

Once you've found a target market to write to, you need a subject, or topic, to write about!

Not all subjects are equal. To find the right subject you must ask, "Why would people in my target market buy my book?"

Given a thousand other things they could buy with their money, and as many other ways they could use their energy rather than studying your words, why would they suffer the expense and make the effort to read what you have written?

Because to do so would bring them a benefit or benefits. Two kinds of benefits are most likely to get them to respond: one that meets a pressing need or one that solves a critical problem.

The benefits can be personal, job- or family-related, or linked to peers or friends. The strongest motivations are achievement, acquisition, or not losing what one already has. And the rewards one can receive from meeting a need or solving a problem? Money, advancement, esteem, respect, happiness, survival, security, order, immortality, leisure, the opportunity to use one's abilities to the fullest, ...

Logically then, the greater the need, the more likely people will want it met. And if the solution to that need comes in book form, the greater the likelihood that they will buy the book. So your TCE success is directly related to finding that crucial need or solution, meeting or solving it on your pages, and telling people with that need that your book exists.

Matching that need to your target market

Every target market has a dozen needs, maybe hundreds or thousands, that it would pay to help meet. For example, some of those needs might concern process or procedure. Those in the market know what must be done but need help doing it or doing it better. Other needs are problems seeking solution. You must find those needs your markets most wants met or those problems it most desperately wants solved.

It makes no sense to write a book full of information nobody wants. Or that nobody will pay much, or anything, to know. Rather, you want to provide eager buyers with information that is so vital, so critical they would be fools not to want it at any reasonable price. And since your plan is to realize a just profit from providing needed information, finding precisely the right subject meets both of your criteria.

Let me suggest two approaches to help you ferret out from the hundreds of possible needs or solutions of your target market that one subject best suited for your book.

One way to find your subject

The first approach presumes an intimate knowledge of the target market and suggests eleven steps to bring the best subject(s) to the surface.

(1) Form a mental picture of a typical person from your target market. Make a list of every problem that person would encounter during an average day that might also be experienced by others from that market. Add special problems from atypical days. Then add every activity, event, or thing that would create stress or frustration in any person from that target market.

(2) Look at that person's total life. How could that life be improved? What problems do others from the target market share? What solutions would help all? What needs must be resolved?

(3) What dreams does your person have? What hopes? How could those be realized? Which of the dreams do all in that market share? Which are the most important? Which, if resolved for one, could be resolved for all?

(4) Why would your typical person from the target market buy your book? To do a better job? To make more money? To improve their family life? To make a lasting contribution to society?

(5) Review the answers to the questions just asked and list a dozen topics, or needs, that your typical person from the target market would buy a book to help meet. Then rearrange that list by urgency or importance of topics, with the most critical first.

(6) Place next to each of those topics a percentage of people in the target market who would see that topic as critical and would likely buy a book about it. Consider the second factor in estimating that percentage: would each person buy their own book or, if bought by one, would the book be passed from person to person? Would the book be bought by the individual or would it be bought for a group of people, to be shared?

(7) If the price of the book were $15, how would that affect the number of buyers? Adjust your percentage of buyers accordingly.

(8) Books don't write and produce themselves, nor is that done instantly. Figure a minimum of two months, with six to ten a more realistic release date from the inception of the idea (particularly for the first publication). How will this alter the order of your list? Which topics won't be critical at that time? Which will be even more urgent?

(9) Now reorder your list. The ideal topic is one desperately desired by every member of your target market. Better yet, one that will be even more desired at the time of publication. The need the book helps meet would be central to the life of the buyer. Every member would not only pay $15 for the book, they would want their own copy. And they would want even more help in that field beyond the book....

(10) Sadly, few books are so fervently awaited or so totally wanted. List the books closest to that ideal first, giving particularly high value to the number of potential buyers.

(11) Now evaluate each book by asking whether it could in fact be written. Is there sufficient information to fill 100-250 pages? Would the contents be worth far more that the $15 you will charge? Would the buyer perceive a personal advantage or benefit from knowing that book's contents?

A second and complementary way

The second approach is more likely to be used by an outsider or one with more casual, or less intimate, knowledge of the target market, though it is an excellent additional exercise for those following the 11-step system just suggested.

Its purpose, again, is to find a subject that everyone in the target market wants to know or know more about. It suggests that you:

(1) Ask those in the market precisely what they desperately want or need to know more about!

(2) See what market-related needs or problems are mentioned in recent, appropriate professional/trade journals and general magazines.

(3) Check newspaper indexes to see what is new, changing, or projected for the future of the target market and about which new information will be critically needed.

(4) See what already exists (or soon will) among the books directed to your market, to see what else is needed, what should be updated, and what must be redone. Check the library stacks and card catalog plus the current *Subject Guide to Books in Print* and *Forthcoming Books*.

The result?

The best possible subject for your TCE book, several subjects for several books (from which the best first book could be chosen), several subjects that could be combined into a super first book, or a wealth of information that could be shared by many means beyond a first book — after that is written and sold!

If you fail to find a subject, look again. There is virtually no target market without a dozen screaming needs begging to be met!

EXAMPLE

My problem now is selecting the right subject for my book about principals. What need or needs would be sufficiently pressing to get those harried souls to quickly cough up $15 to read my words? Nothing less will do.

Let's use the 11-step guide to find and begin to define a topic:

(1) A typical person in my primary target market would be a principal, male or female. Now an administrator, previously a teacher —

some continue teaching a class or two. Probably 30+, more likely in the 40-50 age range. Has a master's degree. Main charge is the total education of the students at his/her school.

The most significant influences on the principal's life come from five sources:

(a) community
(b) school
(c) superintendent/school board
(d) family
(e) other personal concerns:
   advancement
   vocational change
   financial security
   retirement
   recreation

Three additional factors are shared by principals and may affect my topic preference: (a) there is often less interest in advancement than in present performance, in part because the next logical vocational advancement would be to superintendent and not only is that highly selective and requires more schooling, it is not considered desirable by many principals; (b) there is low profit motive as a stimulus for achievement, and (c) creativity is limited by the superintendent as well as by the community (and perhaps church).

Focussing on school, most of a principal's problems or concerns would fall in one of these categories:

faculty	budget	time management
staff	paperwork	innovation
buildings	stress	incentives
grounds	burnout	goals
safety	public relations	teamwork
buses.	books	superintendent
community	organization	moral standard
parents	morale	athletics

(2) Looking at a principal's total life, another huge sector begs attention. High visibility in the community and a position of leadership put stress on the normal conduct of a non-school life, so a second area of concerns might be:

>   maintaining a balance between job and family
>   earning sufficient income to meet present and future needs
>   recreation and outside activities
>   planning for a future beyond principalship
>   avoiding or overcoming burnout in all aspects of life
>   midlife crisis
>   planning for an exciting and fulfilling retirement

(3) Principals' dreams are no different from most others'. They want to lead full, productive, significant lives. If married, be loving spouses; if parents, raise children that represent the best of what they want for all of the children in their schools. If there is one major wish that most others don't share, it is probably to be less visible, less in the public eye, to lead a private life in addition to the public one, to be able to separate "principalship" from their own beings when they want to.

(4) Principals are readers, literate and aware that information and benefits can come from the written word, so they are an ideal book market. They would buy a book if they felt it would give them information, an insight, or guidance in problem-solving, whether related to school or their non-school lives.

(5) Rather than list topics here, it is clear to me that a book or books can be written in one of two areas, or both:

>   (a) about the principal and the school, or
>   (b) about the principal's life outside of the school

What I need to know is how many other books exist in either category, to see if there are needs in each that are unmet in print. So a list will be held in abeyance at this step and prepared after that reference survey is completed.

(6) Books in either category could be seen as critical by the principal, depending on how topics are approached and how well and fully they offer guidance or solutions. As for whether each principal would buy a book, it seems likely that for school issues one book in the district would suffice, to be shared. For personal issues, the book would more likely be bought individually by each principal for personal use.

(7) $15 wouldn't be problem for a book that would likely be paid out of school funds.

(8) A book about life outside of school would be little affected by a later publication date. A few school-related topics would if they are "hot "now" and need resolution quickly.

(9)-(11) More on these later as we further define the topic itself.

Where does that leave us now? With two directions but no firm topic — yet. We're zeroing in but whether we write about "the principal and the school," from some slant, or "the principal's life outside the school" depends very much upon who has written about each before, how often the subject has been in print, how recently, how well known and widely bought the books were, and other such answers.

We will continue the topic refinement in Chapter Six.

Incidentally, where did I find out the above information, not being a principal nor close to the field? Simple. I read indexes of professional magazines for principals, I looked at the subjects included in the *Reader's Guide to Periodical Literature* for all categories touching principals, I reread the job description in Chapter Four, and I asked six principals what problems they currently face at their schools and about which would they buy books for solutions. Under what guise did I ask the principals? Under the dark and mysterious subterfuge of looking for a subject for a coming book to principals! They provided me with the best information.

CUSTOMIZING

In the "T" of the TCE process you "targeted" your market, then you targeted a need of that market.

Now, in the "C" you are going to "customize" your information to meet that specific need for that particular market. Here you will tailor-fit your book, every stitch for a purpose, custom-sewn to one person, for one group. Your book will be written in their language. It will look like books they buy. It will be bound and decorated and illustrated specifically to their tastes. Most important, your book will do one thing and do it fully: meet that need or solve that problem. And it will do it solely with that buyer in mind.

The next nine chapters talk about customizing your book specifically to your tightly-targeted market.

6 MEETING THAT NEED THROUGH A BOOK: CHECKING, MEASURING, AND FITTING

Having found and defined a specific need that you can meet or a solution you can provide in your book, it's imperative to do three more things: (1) see if that need can be, or soon will be able to be, met by someone else's book, or several; (2) develop a purpose statement, a working question, and all necessary secondary questions to serve as the basic organizational structure of your book, and (3) determine whether there is sufficient material to fill a book's pages.

In other words, next is the necessary checking, measuring, and fitting to see whether a book is the appropriate means for sharing your information. As important, can it be prepared the TCE way? And will it bring you profits?

What if a book isn't the proper or best way? Maybe a different means of information dissemination is. We'll discuss that in the next chapter. Best you know now before investing more time, effort, and money in a book that isn't, to you, fully worth writing!

Is this need being met by one or many other books?

Why write a book that already exists, or soon will? Fortunately, in the computer age you needn't guess. Just dig out the facts.

The results of your research will pay you handsomely since what you find you will use again and again in your TCE quest.

First, go to your library and find your subject in the card catalog. List every sub-category by which related information is also found. Article indexes, like the *Reader's Guide to Periodical Literature*, can also show related sub-categories.

Then, armed with the topic heading and related headings where you might also find valuable material, begin your resource compilation. You are actually seeking two kinds of information: (1) that which directly addresses the need you wish to help meet through your book, and (2) related information about that need and similar needs.

A quick example of how the latter might be used, beyond indicating source books for reference during your later research. Let's say that your intent is to write a book called *How To Create a Better School*. But when you check the library you find many good, general books that explain just that. Yet none specifically addresses particular kinds or levels of school. A possible result? Your new book might be called *How To Build a Better Middle School!*

Here are some steps to take to see if the need has already been adequately covered, what other books exist about it in print (or soon will), what your book may have to contain to be competitive or sufficiently comprehensive, and what other books about closely related topics are available.

(1.) Go to the library of a major university and investigate the need for, feasibility, and cost of a computer search. To keep the cost reasonable and the results useful, work closely with the librarian to identify precisely what information you want and by which categories it can be found. Also see if an articles search can be done at the same time, to save money and time and to facilitate your contents research later.

(2.) If a computer search is not done, or to supplement it, check the following library sources for books about your subject: the card catalog (including microfiche and microfilm listings), the stacks themselves to find books either unlisted or poorly titled (for your purposes), the current *Subject Guide To Books In Print* (which lists the books published in the past few years, each with the publisher's name and address), the current *Forthcoming Books*, formerly *Forthcoming Books in Print* (which lists books that will be released in the coming six months, with a short description of each and the publisher from which they can be purchased), any Library of Congress subject index listing that is available, plus of course the bibliographies of those books found. On the long shot, you might see if any booklets or pamphlets are hiding in the vertical index or file. There's also *Wilson's Vertical File Index*. Ask your librarian for help, if you need it!

(3.) Divide the books found into two groups: (a) those in direct competition with your book, that either meet the need you wish to meet or are close enough in theme that a person in your target market may buy them instead of your book, and (b) those about related or similar subjects that aren't directly competitive but which you will want to consult for research.

(4.) For the second group, prepare an annotated bibliography from the information you have at hand. (It isn't necessary at this point to see the actual books.) List the author or editor, full title, publisher, date of publication, and where you can find the book for later consultation (if you know). Add to that anything you know or can deduce from a catalog listing about that book's contents as it relates to your topic.

(5.) For the first group, those which compete with your book, you need to know far more. Here you must study both content and form to see the market standard, to serve as a guide to what a comprehensive book about this topic contains, and to see what your book needs. (If the competition isn't as good as it might be or as comprehensive as it should be, that can provide you with an excellent marketing advantage. Alas, you must study the rest to know that.) This is what you need to know about every book in this group:

(a) author(s) or editor(s)

(b) other books written by the same author(s) or editor(s)

(c) full title (including sub-title[s])

(d) publisher (with address, if small press)

(e) date of publication

(f) date of copyright and by whom

(g) number of editions or printings and the dates of each

(h) whether the book is part of a series; if so, information about the series, its theme, items (a)-(c) and (e)-(g) above about each book

(i) form of binding of all forms of this book: cloth, paper, spiral, etc.

(j) cost of each of the books in (i)

(k) number of pages; number in each chapter or section

(l) why the book was written — check the introduction or first chapter where the purpose statement or working question often appear; more on these later in this chapter

(m) kinds and number of illustrations used and the sources of each, where identified

(n) number and kind of charts, graphs, maps, etc. and whether each was prepared for this book or is a reprint from another source. If the latter, what source?

(o) number and kind of how-to guides

(p) whether the book is designed for classroom use. If so, explain. For example, does it contain a summary and exercises after each chapter?

(q) does it contain a foreword? Who wrote it?

(r) are there testimonials in the book? Where? By whom?

(s) are other products sold through the book? How? Is a price list printed? Where does it appear? Describe each of the products in detail.

(t) does the book mention future editions or books about this or a related topic? How? Give full details.

(u) describe the bibliography; does it list books only? Articles? Other information sources? What is the most recent item listed? How many items are listed?

(v) does it include a glossary? Table of contents? Index? List of illustrations? Dedication? Introduction?

(w) describe the appendix, if any. What is listed? How many pages long is each item?

(x) is the book current? Out-of-date? Incomplete? Misdirecting? Evaluate the book in these and any other terms that will identify its position in the body of literature about this field.

(y) where was this book reviewed? What did reviewers say about it? In retrospect, are they accurate?

By studying other books designed and published to meet the need in detail, you can see how your book must differ (if at all) to compete profitably. Even if other available publications don't directly address the same need, a close review of their structure and content will provide a model to be followed, modified, or ignored. Some questions that such a review might provoke are:

(1.) How can you slant or direct your focus to create a new, different, better, more desirable book? Or is any or all of that necessary? Said in a different way, how can you make your book, among the others now or soon to be available, sufficiently unique and wanted to be bought by at least 10% of the target market at $15 a copy?

(2.) How could this book be better tied to the target market? What is unavailable — at all, at this level, in this way — to the desired buyer that this book might provide? How could the book's unique features be made known to those who might buy it?

(3.) How could you increase the perceived value of the book? A foreword by a well-known expert in the field? A co-author with wider recognition? More or different how-to guides and checklists? A companion workbook? Testimonials on the front or back cover, or both?

(4.) What other means of information dissemination might you use to increase your sharing of this information while also increasing your profits? (More on that in Chapter Seven.)

Developing the organizational structure of your book

In-depth research about competition and other, related resources is crucial to finding your book's unique core and its selling "hook."

Still, there's something even more important to finding that unique core. You must know precisely what you hope to achieve with your book. What is its purpose?

So the next step is to develop a purpose statement, a working question, and all the secondary questions necessary to creating your book's basic organizational structure.

A purpose statement

This is as uncomplicated as it sounds. Explain, in one sentence, the purpose of your proposed book. "The purpose of this book is ..." But one sentence only. If you need two or three, you don't know precisely what your book will be about.

It may be uncomplicated but it isn't always easy to zero in that tightly. But it must be done, and the earlier the better. It simplifies the research and writing task and gives you a measuring tool as you work.

Woe to the writer who heads into the word jungle to write a book, thinking to research and write the definitive study of the gnat, only to discover that what he really wants to tell is how to catch a hippo. He's in the wrong woods with the wrong tools for the wrong reason, wasting too much time reporting very wrong facts.

A working questions

Now rewrite that one-sentence statement into a working question.

From "The purpose of this book is to explain how to catch a hippopotamus." you would write "How does one catch a hippopotamus?"

Why? Because your book answers that question. By doing so it achieves its purpose. If it doesn't, why bother? Your reader expects to find out how to catch a hippo from the title and everything that your promotion promises. Anything less angers the buyer and creates true distress for you.

The working question is the plumb line that all in the book touches. It is the gauge by which items are included, trimmed, stretched, or deleted. If the material does not tell how to catch a hippo, directly or indirectly, it is material for somebody else's book — or yours later when you write another book that it addresses.

Secondary questions

Secondary questions flow from the primary question. They usually begun with "who, what, why, where, when, or how," the working tools of journalists.

"Where could you catch a hippo?"
"How is it done?"
"When?"
"What tools would you need?
"Who could do it? What skills would it require?"
"Why would you even want to try?"

Most writers can think of 30 or 40 key questions that virtually ask themselves once the working question is posed. To understand the answer to the working question fully it's necessary to understand the secondary questions.

So write every such question that comes to mind. Spend time here. Put them all down. And then rearrange the questions in some sensible order. If your book is historical in theme, list the questions chronologically. If its theme is how to catch a hippo, consider a developmental order. If it's a how-to action book based on others' experiences, perhaps list case studies in either a chronological or developmental format. You figure out what works best to achieve your purpose.

What comes from defining a purpose statement, putting it in working question form, writing down the secondary questions that must be answered to fully answer the working question, then putting those secondary questions in some sensible order? A book outline. Not in marble, not definitive with its parts immobile, but a solid book outline that will give structure and a spine to all that follows.

Usually the secondary questions, reduced to key words, become chapter headings. And the words that answer secondary questions become bricks that hold that framework, that outline, in place and provide the substance, ideas, dreams, humor, and expression of the book.

Each chapter answers its secondary question. Cumulatively, they answer the working question, and by doing so your purpose, expressed in the purpose statement, can be achieved.

That achievement, in terms of your book, is the reason for its existence and for the hard work and dedication you put into its creation.

In terms of the TCE approach, you must go a step beyond simply creating a book. To increase its market value, success is closely related to (a) how closely and clearly the working question matches the target market's need; (b) how you respond to that question, and (c) how well you inform that target market that you are asking that question, how fully you are answering it, and why it should care.

Sufficient material for a book?

Later you will gather your material for your book. Here you are further defining the book's purpose and seeing how it will be unique. You also want to know if you'll be able to fill 100, 200, 300 — you pick the length — pages of solid, valuable information.

Mostly this is done by seeing what others included in books similar to yours and estimating if you can do the same. Often the beginner is certain that there's no more than 30 pages of material anywhere in the world, while the veteran writer, looking at the same supply, wonders how he or she can possibly fit it into a salable length!

How long is long enough? As Abraham Lincoln said when asked how tall a man should be, "A man must be tall enough for his feet to touch the ground." The same for a book. It must be long enough to achieve its purpose.

Since one of the purposes of TCE books is to sell at a profitable cost, most people have certain expectations related to page count (or at least book bulk) and what they will pay for it. So as a very rough guide, unless the contents are truly singular and worth a clearly perceived fortune (in which case any length will do) shoot for a minimum of about 125 pages, better 200. Beyond that it doesn't matter much.

Then your task is to estimate if you have information, or can get it, that will result in 125-200+ pages of copy, some of which is front and back matter, illustrations, chapter headings, and other elements unrelated to research or body copy. If you don't come close, you have some choices: abandon the book, find what is missing, or sell the information by other means. This is a good time to guesstimate.

After the example we will talk about that last choice: selling what you know by means other than a book.

EXAMPLE

I still have a key problem unresolved. I found a market need — two of them! Until I make a choice I can't tightly define my book topic nor create the purpose statement, working question, or secondary questions.

So I must focus first on whether this book will be about "principals and school" or "principals and their lives outside of school." The best way to do that is by seeing what is already in print about either subject.

My next step is the library. Actually three libraries — one from a small town, a second at a community college, and the third at a major state university. I find a wealth of information at the third, some 160 books in total. What follows are examples from sub-categories of "principal" or "principalship" listed at that institution:

Examples from the five-book total at the library under "Teacher-Principal Relationship":

> Andrew, Loyd D., et. al., *Administrator's handbook for improving faculty morale*, Phi Delta Kappa, 1985, 70 pages.
> Antoniswami, Anthony, *Analysis of lay and religious principals' and teachers' perceptions of leader behavioral style and organizational climate in Catholic schools*, Ph.D. thesis (Catholic University of America), 1983, 120.
> Sargent, James C., *Organizational climate of high schools: a study of principal and staff perceptions*, 1967, 30.

Examples from the eight-book total under "High School Principals":

> *The senior high school principalship*, NASSP, 1978.
> Molitor, Leo T., Jr., *Size and Substance of the evaluation component* in *high school administration*, Ph.D. thesis (U.C.S.B.), 1981, 205.
> Trump, J. Lloyd and Lois S. Karasik, *The first 55 years*, NASSP, 1967,28.
> Wood, Charles L., *The secondary principal: manager and supervisor*, Allyn and Bacon, 1979, 353.
> Dean, Joan, *Managing the secondary school* (in Great Britain), Croom Helm, 1985, 239.

Examples from the 81-book total under "School Superintendents and Principals," citing those that directly mention principals in the title:

> Burden, Larry and R. L. Whitt, *The community school principal — new horizons*, Pendell Pub., 1973, 250.
> Davis, Frank G., *Guidance manual for principals*, McGraw-Hill, 1949, 71.
> Frank, John, *School principal: handbook of evaluation guidelines*, Parker Pub., 1978, 251.
> Gross, Neal C. and Anne E. Trash, *The sex factor and the management of schools*, Wiley, 1976, 279.
> Jacobsen, Paul P., James D. Logsdon, and Robert R. Wiegman, *The principalship: new perspective*, Prentice-Hall, 1973, 499.
> Kyte, George C., *The Principal at Work*, Ginn and Co., 1941, 495.
> Patterson, Barbara B., *Perceptions of efficiency in effective and ineffective principals*, Ph.D. thesis (U.C.S.B.), 1984, 201.
> Strother, P.B. (ed.), *The role of principal*, Phi Delta Kappa, 1983, 239.

Examples from the 53 sub-titles under "School Superintendents and Principals," such as "Case Studies," "Guidelines," "Laws/Legal Statues," "Salaries/Pensions," etc.:

> Basset, G.W., *Australian primary schools and their principals*, Harcourt, Brace, 1984, 247.
> Kelley, Edgar A., *Improving climate leadership techniques for principals*, NASSP, 1980, 73.
> Nolte, M. Chester, *How to survive as principal: the legal dimension*, 1983, 245.
> Drake, Thelbert L. and William H. Roe, *The principalship*, Macmillan, 1986, 480.
> Saxer, Richard W., *Perspectives on the changing role of the principal*, Thomas, 1968, 312.

Examples from the 17-book total under "Elementary School Principals":

> Diaz, Tony C., *Role expectations of the elementary school principal in school community relations*, E.D. thesis (U. of Houston), 1976,149.
> Lietz, Jeremy L., *The elementary principal's role in special education*, Thomas, 1982, 173.

Two things are obvious.

One, superintendents are often linked to principals in book titles and subject categories. So I might think of combining the two in my book. Or writing another book about a similar topic, specifically customizing it to superintendents. At the very least I must include superintendents in my selling market for the principals' book, somewhere between the targeted market and the expanded general market.

Two, every book I found on the shelf, new or old, was about the principal and school. Not a one directly acknowledged, at least in the title, that the principal has a private, non-school life. Which suggests two obvious questions: (1) is there need for another book about principals and their schools? and (2) is there need at all for a book about principals and their private lives?

Further research may give clear answers to each question — or not. Right now I need to make at least a tentative choice of book topics, leaving that choice open to reversal should information later found so warrant it.

My thinking, based on what I've read and heard about principals and what I find in other books directed to them, is summarized this way:

> (1) there will probably always be need for another book about principals and their schools. But the field is crowded now, new writers will continue to work it, a new book will have to fight for attention, and one would likely have to focus on a particular level or type of school, thus reducing the selling market.
>
> (2) principals are people and a book that focussed on that would stand alone, or at least would stand out. The field is empty, a new book would get noticed, and there is probably more that principals share in their private lives than separates them wherever they teach. I'd have 100% of the principal market to sell!

(3) my decision now is to write the book about principals and their private lives. I will expand upon that theme with spinoff items in writing and speaking. Then I'll see whether it is prudent to remain in that field or redirect my energies, using my mailing list and recognition, to write in the "principal and school" field.

Completing the 5-step guideline

In summarizing the results of the five-step guideline, it wasn't necessary to make a computer search since my topic choice had no books about it in any of the three libraries I visited nor could I find a book about "principals and their life outside of school" *per se* listed in the past decade in the *Subject Guide To Books In Print*. Nor did the current *Forthcoming Books* show anything on the publishing horizon. Finally, a check of bibliographies of the larger and more thorough books about principals and principalship revealed no such tome.

There was no two-division grouping of books. All were in the second category, about related or similar subjects — about principals on the job. They were useful in telling me what principals did, or should do, and in showing me the kinds of books that principals read: their length, form, and price. Even that isn't too helpful. These are "business books" and principals read them because they are the choices. A book about their personal lives could be far different. Therefore the detailed listing in (5) isn't really applicable either except to indicate that principals are accustomed to books more academic in tone and form. Elements of that genre, like footnotes and an index, while unlikely to be included in the kind of book I have in mind, might be expected by this group and make my book more salable.

And the 4-question review

My book will in itself be different and new. Other than being excellent in content and appealing in form, how do I make it worth far more than the $15 I want to charge for it? And how do I sell it to more than 10% of my target market?

By making it speak directly to the needs, hopes, fears, desires, frustrations, and dreams of every contemporary principal. As important, by making it fact-filled, practical, and to the point. Principals aren't idlers or daydreamers; they want applicable information that works. They also want examples, people like themselves from whom they can learn and with whom they can laugh. They may want lists, guidelines, goals, inspiration, techniques. The book must read easily and well, free from academic jargon yet in the educated tone principals expect.

Testimonials will help once the book is out. However impervious principals may feel themselves to such selling techniques, they are followers as well as leaders. Opinion moves them too. Peals of praise like "Principals as throbbing, living souls! Somebody finally noticed!" or "Chuck full of fun and common sense!" or "Haven't enjoyed anything this much since I rang that last spring bell!" Cartoons well placed, funny, and emphasizing a point might give the book an edge, in contrast to the usual drab educational primer.

There are several associations and most principals usually belong to at least one — more on this later. But they can be used to make the members aware of the book, through a review, display ads, mailing list rental, etc.

Probably the biggest selling point of this book is that it alone talks about the humanness of principals. That focus must be emphasized. The simplest of examples, one faced by every teacher in a small town: how to go out for a social drink and not be paraded as a disgraceful public drunk by the Board of Education (members of which were in the same pub)! Nobody is discussing the private lives of principals.

And how else might this information be shared other than a book? I will look at that in the next chapter, but the first things that come to mind would be speeches or seminars to gatherings of principals. Articles could be developed from the book before and after it is published. Perhaps tapes, audio and video, might expand on the theme, and a newsletter might be eagerly welcomed by many in the field.

Developing the organizational structure

First I need a purpose statement for the book. What is the book to do? To show principals how to lead full, challenging lives while they are working and after they retire. To do that lovingly. To help them leave their mark personally as well as professionally. And to do all of this within the context in which they live and work. So my purpose statement, one sentence long, would read this way:

> The purpose of this book is to share with principals ways by which they can serve their schools, families, and communities with love and lasting distinction while also leading balanced, challenging, full lives during and after their principalships.

From that purpose statement it is a simple switch to the interrogatory mode for a working question:

> How can principals serve their schools, families, and communities with love and lasting distinction while also leading balanced, challenging, full lives during and after their principalships?

Some secondary questions that first come to mind are:

(1) what are the ways by which these ideals can be attained?
(2) which leads to which benefit? Or are "balanced, challenging, full lives" the composite goal?
(3) are these sought by every principal? Or are we writing for certain principals in certain conditions?
(4) what are the components of a balanced life? What is balanced in a principal's context?
(5) challenging in what way? vocationally? academically? spiritually?
(6) some would contend that serving the school is a full life, and that by doing that well all else will follow. Is that true?
(7) what might other definitions of a full life outside of school be?

plus 1000 questions more.

I still know too little about what principals want outside their school lives. I don't have a handle on their needs yet. In subsequent steps I will research more and do some test marketing. That will help me zero in far faster and with greater certainty on the best secondary questions from which I can develop a working outline. Patience!

Sufficient material for a book?

This is a concern since there is almost nothing in print to draw from. Where will I find material to fill these pages?

From the books about principals and their schools rare references are made to their non-school lives. Those can be drawn from, as can articles sometimes touching this topic. But most of the information will come from interviews with actual, practicing principals and other experts about the aspects of private life discussed as they apply to principals. It can be obtained as an investigative journalist does: find people, call them, explain what I am doing, arrange interviews, and share the information gathered.

Is there enough for 120-200+ pages? As long as there are private life issues of interest to principals, the principals themselves to interview, and enough money and time for me to gather this information, filling the pages should be no problem.

7 MEETING THAT NEED THROUGH OTHER INFORMATION DISSEMINATION NEEDS

If you accept the premise that "if you know something that others will pay to know, they will pay to know it many ways and by many means," you must now ask by which ways can you best share your information?

Up to this point I have assumed that a book would be the most appropriate means of sharing, but it is time for you to test that assumption about your subject. And to identify, prioritize, and integrate the development of the other means while your book is being prepared, promoted, and published.

The path one follows here is nearly identical to that of Chapter Six. Except that first you must (1) identify the most appropriate means, then (2) see if somebody else is already, or soon will be, meeting those needs by those means, (3) develop a specific purpose statement, working question, and secondary questions for each means pursued, (4) see if there is sufficient material to create the sharing by that means, and (5) design a general working schedule for the creation and development of these means in relationship to the book.

Is a book the best way at all? Is it time to re-evaluate?

While assuming that a book is the best way to share your information, I know that that isn't always the case. (Still, for the purposes of this book, I will continue to make that assumption since for the vast majority of its readers it is so. For those for whom another means would be the best primary sharing tool, use the remainder of this text as a rough guideline for the other means and a more complete guideline for developing a book as a secondary tool.)

For all, now is the time to test the assumption before going any further.

When, for example, might a book not be the best primary sharing tool? The choreography of a ballet, while possible to explain on illustrated charts, would better be seen on a video. The score of a symphony comes in printed form; how it is performed by a certain orchestra would better be transmitted by audio cassette, record, or disk. To share facts or an opinion nationwide quickly can't be done by book. Yet a book would be perfect for a retrospective analysis or an explanation in depth.

What is clear is that most information is well shared by many means. What determines the primary means is the purpose of that particular sharing, time, and the economics of each means.

Comparing the information dissemination means

One straightforward way of getting a global sense of the relationship between a book and other information dissemination means is to list them, then ask whether each means is appropriate (by a yes/no response and/or by assigning each a scaled, evaluative number, say 1-5, as to its relative appropriateness), and finally by comparing them, perhaps listing them in descending order of appropriateness.

Other than a book, what means of information dissemination are most often used to share information the TCE way? In no particular order: articles, newsletters, reports, talks, speeches, classes, seminars/workshops, audio cassettes, video cassettes, consulting, film, radio, TV, and, most recently, computer software.

A comparison chart might look like this:

Means	Appropriate?	Rank of appropriateness
book		
articles		
newsletters		
reports		
talks		
speeches		
seminars/workshops		
classes		
audio cassettes		
video cassettes		
consulting		
film		
radio		
TV		
computer software		

Another way to evaluate means, contents, markets, and more...

Let me suggest a more playful approach to thinking about your book's subject and how it might be more widely shared, developed, and marketed. I call it topic-spoking and I develop it far more fully in *Empire-Building by Writing and Speaking* (see information about this book on the last page). Here, let's simply introduce and explain the concept, then give an example.

First you draw a topic-spoking diagram, like this:

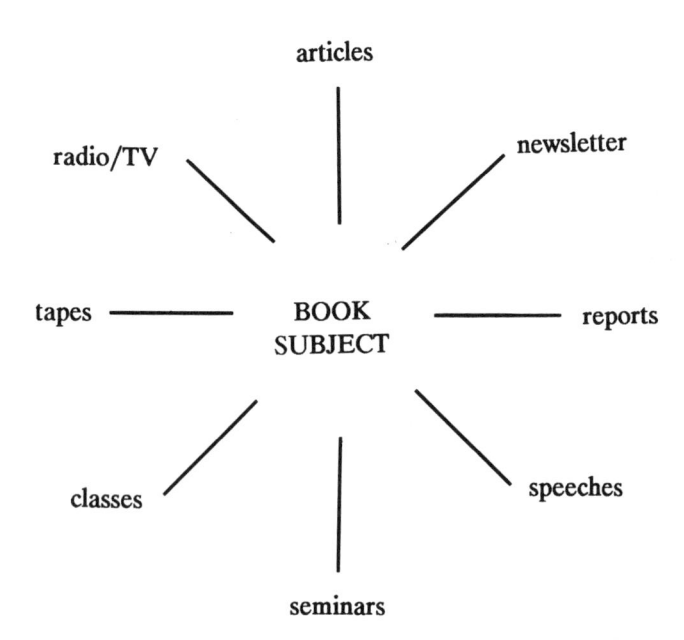

```
                    articles
                       |
    radio/TV           |         newsletter
          \            |           /
           \           |          /
            \          |         /
   tapes  ————    BOOK SUBJECT    ————  reports
            /          |         \
           /           |          \
          /            |           \
    classes            |            speeches
                       |
                    seminars
```

Then you write the book's subject in the center of the diagram, as I've done above. You might then put the most appropriate information dissemination means at the end of each of the spokes. Use or add the spokes that you need. (A book as a means is excluded here because the book topic is in the center and we are seeking other, non-book means by which we can share the information.)

This is simply another way of doing what the comparison chart does, to select from many possibilities those means most likely to be useful and profitable for this particular subject. The chart sets up a ranking of appropriateness. That can be done on the topic-spoking diagram by putting the most appropriate in the top (or 12 o'clock position), the next most important next (at, say the 2 o'clock spot), and so on. The visual value of the diagram is that you can see each means in relationship to the others and begin, perhaps, to see ways that various means might be combined to provide even more or better ways of sharing. A quick example: combining articles or columns into an anthology (in book form) to be sold at speeches and talks.

Then ask at each spoke how that topic might be shared by this means. What product or service could be developed to explain the topic that way? Which already exist? How might you build on them? How might that means be combined with another? Which new ways might you create? You might also make columns below the diagram to note your ideas.

The same format can be used many ways. Let's say that you want to sell this book to other markets besides principals. You write in the center "Other Markets For Principal Book" and at the end of the spokes you write down any such market that comes to mind.

Or you want to begin thinking about what this book might contain — its chapters or internal structure. You write in the center "Book Chapters: Principal's Life After School" and at the end of the spokes you write down anything that you think the book should cover.

Here's a fourth game to play with topic-spoking, suggested with the rest as a way of getting you to see the whole self-publishing and book-centering project in its fullest context. One of the main themes of the book might be to show that principals are much more than just school administrators and that much of their greater sense of fulfillment and happiness would come from identifying and building on those other facets in addition to the principalship. Therefore, to begin to identify the other things a principal might be you would put in the center of the diagram "Principal as a ..." and at the end of the spokes, the other things he/she might explore for fuller growth.

In the example at the end of this chapter all four diagrams have been completed. Some are directly applicable now, in thinking about other means of sharing the book's subject. Others related more to subsequent chapters, but are developed now to show you but four of the many, many ways topic-spoking can be used to stimulate the mind and create a fuller, more useful, and more profitable product.

Tightly-Targeted Markets

Is somebody else already meeting the need by the appropriate means?

No guesswork here. If you've identified some means as appropriate ways to share your information beyond the book, before you invest much time or money you want to know who else is plowing those fields and how bountiful is their harvest. So speculation is replaced by some digging of your own.

You've already been to the library and know where to find books on the topic, plus you know the related headings. That should help you use the guides listed below. In addition, always ask the reference librarian for other, current research materials.

>   **ARTICLES**: in magazines, check the *Reader's Guide to Periodical Literature* for articles in commercial publications, as well as equivalent indexes for articles in the various academic disciplines most closely related to your topic. For articles in newspapers, see newspaper indexes both from major cities, such as *The New York Times Index,* or those of newspapers nearest to or most interested in the topic.

>   **NEWSLETTERS**: check the *Newsletters Directory*.

>   **REPORTS**: Hard to locate. Find groups most likely to sell or release reports about the topic. Often they are trade or professional associations, so to first find that group, then know what they publish, see the annual *Encyclopedia of Associations*. Also very helpful is the Associations' *Publications in Print*, with a subject index showing reports, pamphlets, cassettes, etc. as well as the cost of each. On the widest scale, check the current *Yearbook of International Organizations*.

>   **SPEECHES**: it is very difficult to find out who is speaking about what. Major speeches are sometimes reported in the monthly magazine *Vital Speeches of the Day*; some of those and others appear in the annual book, *Representative American Speeches of* (current year). Another way is to check the topic category and listing titles of the speakers in the annual *National Speakers Association Membership Directory*.

SEMINARS: there is no central source, so you must check catalogs of seminars offered by colleges and universities, plus see what is offered to your specific market through professional or trade associations or to or through firms employing members of the potential market. Public seminars are often advertised through newspapers or by direct mail.

CLASSES: get a current schedule of the institutions where classes about the subject might be taught.

AUDIO TAPES: for specific, current CD, LP, and tapes available, check the monthly *Schwann, Compact Disc Catalog* (under "Spoken and Miscellaneous") as well as *Schwann-2, Record and Tape Guide* (see particularly "SpokenWord," "Documentary," and "Educational.") The *Directory of Spoken-Word Audio Cassettes*, by Gerald McKee, was last published in 1983. For a complete guide to A-V reference periodicals and books, see *AVMP: Audio Video Market Place* (current year), published by Bowker.

VIDEO TAPES: the best here is *The Video Source Book*, an annual with some 53,000 program listings. With subject, title, and category breakdowns, you may want to check "Business/Industry," "General Interest/Education," "Health/Science," and "How-To/Instructional." Also available are *The Video Directory* and *The Complete Guide to Videocassette Movies*.

FILM: check the *Educational Film Locator*, which has both subject and title listings. Extremely comprehensive, a joint effort of the University Film Centers and Bowker.

RADIO: two source books that tell what shows have been on the radio in the past, see Vincent Terrace's *Radio's Golden Years* and John Dunning's *Tune in Yesterday: The Ultimate Encyclopedia of Old-Time Radio, 1925-76*.

TV: again, Vincent Terrace, this time the *Complete Encyclopedia of Television Programs, 1947-79*.

What do you do once you have the basic information? Follow the steps of Chapter Six, particularly (3)-(5) and the following (1)-(3), focussing each

Tightly-Targeted Markets

time on the information means in question. The idea is to see how much information is available about your subject by each means, how it is presented, how it is organized and packaged, how it is sold, its appearance and cost — in short, everything you need to know to do the same.

Do you really need a new purpose statement, working question, and secondary questions?

The beauty of basic research is that information in one field or shared by one means can quickly be applied to another field or other means. An article telling how to cook quiche provides information that can easily be used in a book, in a video script, or for a cooking class or seminar. So what you have already found out about your subject from books will serve as a solid base to share other ways. Why then would you need a new purpose statement and all that follows?

A different kind of sharing format brings with it a change in purpose and style, though often the differences are slight.

If the purpose statement of the article about cooking quiche is "to explain to readers, through words and two illustrations, the ingredients required and steps taken to prepare and cook quiche," then the purpose statement for a video with roughly the same intent would be different. It might be "to explain and show how to prepare and cook quiche, then to show, by using five different ingredients, how the viewer could convert the basic recipe into ten different quiches." The difference centers around "telling" in the article and "showing and telling" in the video.

With a different purpose statement comes a different working question and some different secondary questions. So you must develop these organizational tools for each means.

Is there sufficient material for each means you wish to pursue?

Again, like a book, here you can only estimate. But it's hard to imagine that if you have sufficient information to write a book you wouldn't have far more than you need to create most of the other means, such as writing an article, report, radio script, or a notes for a talk.

The one area where attention must particularly be paid concerns newsletters. Often they branch off and build from the book. That is, potential subscribers have read the book and now want more, new, vital information about the same or a very closely related subject. If possible, this can be a huge source of income and a vibrant core of an empire. But sometimes a subject is only one book deep. To try to milk that book for newsletters would be useless if the cow was dry.

Designing an integrated schedule of other means around a book

The purpose of identifying the other means that you may pursue at this stage is to (1) reduce preparation and marketing time for each means, (2) prevent any confusing overlap, and (3) increase your total income from all means.

What you are selling, remember, is expertise. As you establish that by one means, your displayed expertise also deserves attention in other ways. For example, who is a better candidate to speak about a subject than the person who wrote the book?

So here you take the most appropriate means from your earlier chart and see when they would best be developed as you write your book.

Let me share my own system, and biases, here. I like to talk with others about a topic as I put a book together. But I like to get paid to do that too. So as I formulate the premises of my book and gather examples, I create a seminar at the same time. Simultaneously, while I'm researching particular aspects of a topic, I gather additional information for very specific articles.

As you can see by my rather simple schemata below, I start first by giving seminars through the extended education system. That allows me to put my concept into words, share it with paying listeners, and hear their questions and ideas, which in turn add to my knowledge and sharpen the contents of my book. At the same time I query about articles, following up positive responses with tailor-made pieces for those pages.

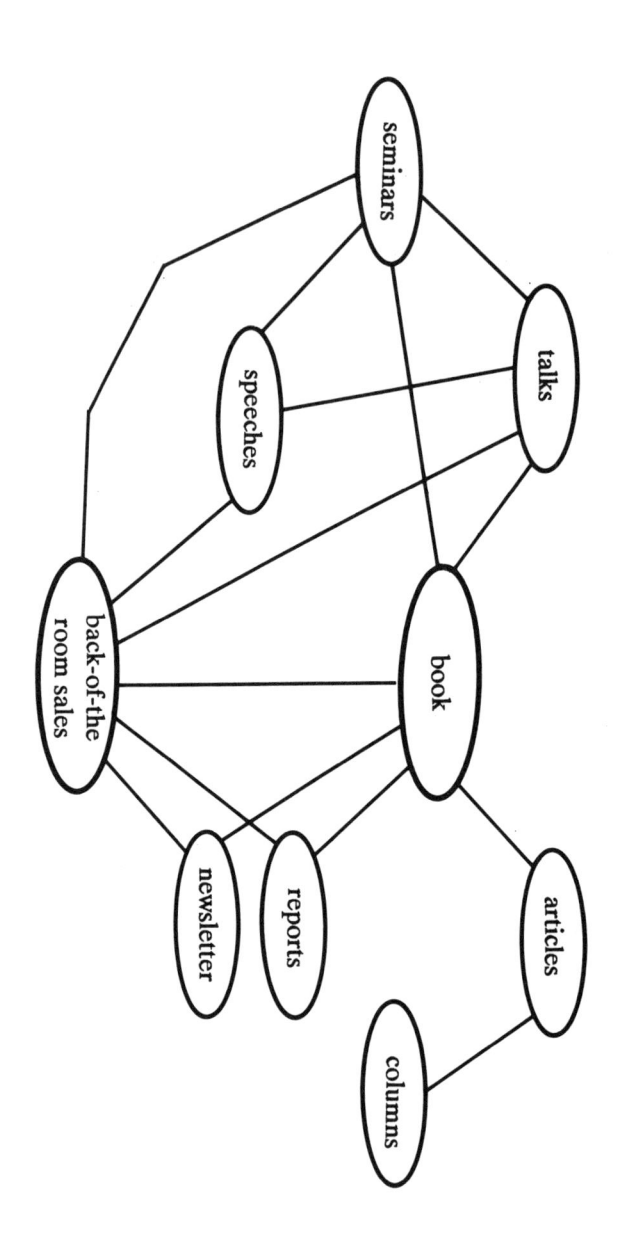

- seminars
- talks
- speeches
- back-of-the-room sales
- book
- newsletter
- reports
- articles
- columns

Somewhat later I write the book, and after it is published I sell it to many of those who attend the seminars that I still offer, as well as to the previous attendees, whose names I have kept.

From the book I produce a half-dozen or so more articles. When these appear in print I include, in the biographical data with my name, information about how the book can be bought.

At some point fairly early on I develop an audio cassette series of the seminar, with the same in-class workbook, and this is made available to seminar participants, book buyers, and libraries. It also serves as a "demo" tape for groups or companies that want to book me as a speaker about that topic.

Speeches are generally sought about the time the book is published, as a result of the publishing promotion, the articles, the tapes, or because a seminar participant wants me to share information with his/her organization or company. At some of those speeches the book and/or tape series are made available after the presentation as back-of-the-room products. At others, they are bought in bulk when I'm booked and given to every participant.

Somewhere along the way, as I become more knowledgeable about the topic, consulting begins, often the result of a person having read my book or heard the seminar, the tape, or a speech and wanting to apply the concept or adapt it to another problem.

Finally, while I don't produce newsletters (because they are simply too time-consuming), if I were to do so I'd begin after the book was out. My best market would be all of the clients who ordered the book or tape or attended the seminar or a speech, plus those who had contacted me about the topic.

The early income from the seminars and tapes helps pay initial expenses of research and book production, plus some of the promotion. And when the book is ready to be sold to my market, I also have a tape series and a seminar to promote on the same flyer, plus a notation of my availability for speaking or consulting. Thus I'm selling one information core five ways, each costing me 20% of what it would cost to market separately. And I've helped scare off competition by planting myself firmly in each of the key fields before anyone can take the book concept and develop products from it.

I nibble at the sides of my market with seminars and articles as I build up my information pool. Then I use my book as the primary full-market penetration tool. I sell the book hard the TCE way. And I wind up doubling income from all the other products and services that build on the same information and are mentioned in the same promotions.

That's really the "E" of TCE, for EXPANDED. If people will buy your information one way, they will buy it many ways and by many means. I will expand upon this in the third section of this book. But now is the time for you to do your groundwork and plant the seeds for profits by other means.

I've explained my thinking and the way I design a simple sketch to integrate other means into my book development. You must do this your way for your topic. Or not do it all— at the very likely loss of considerable income at every facet of your subject's creation and development.

EXAMPLE

How could I interest principals in my subject? Would it be through a book or by one of the many other means of information dissemination?

My gut reaction? A book is best. Principals are academics first, got to their position through teaching, look to the written word for answers and guidance, are literate, can afford books, and are accustomed to ordering or buying them. So I see the other means as secondary— but not unimportant.

By which of the other means might I expect principals to hear about and become interested in my "whole life" or "life beyond school" theme? Time for a comparison chart!

Means	Appropriate?	Rank of appropriateness
articles	yes	2
column	yes	3
newsletters	yes	6
reports	yes	5
talks/speeches	yes	1
seminars/workshops	yes	4
classes	no	
audio cassettes	no	
video cassettes	no	
consulting	maybe	7
film	no	
radio	no	
TV	no	
computer software	no	

Let's also look at these means by topic-spoking

Earlier in this chapter I explained this approach so let me now show and explain how the four topic-spoking diagrams might look.

The first asks by which means might I best develop this book's topic. So I have put the topic in the center and the various means on the spokes, in the order (from 12 o'clock, clockwise) in which I think they would be most useful. Then I ask myself the questions earlier posed, plus others. And to keep track of my responses I put the spoke headings below the diagram so I can make notations.

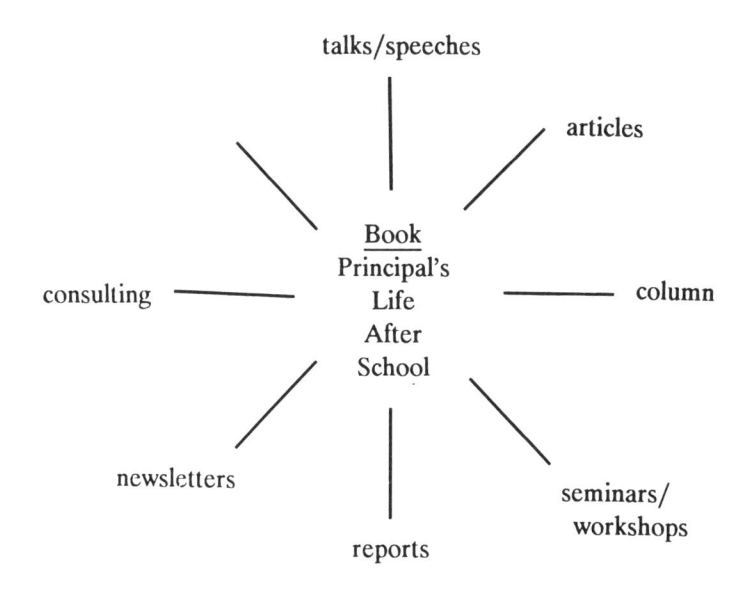

```
              talks/speeches
                    |
                    |           articles
                     \         /
                      \       /
                       Book
consulting ——— Principal's ——— column
                       Life
                     After
                     School
                      /       \
                     /         \
                    /           \
              newsletters      seminars/
                    |          workshops
                    |
                 reports
```

Diverging strictly from the "other means" theme of this chapter to expand this topic-spoking idea, how might the second example appear, where I attempt to spoke "other markets for the book for principals"?

Tightly-Targeted Markets

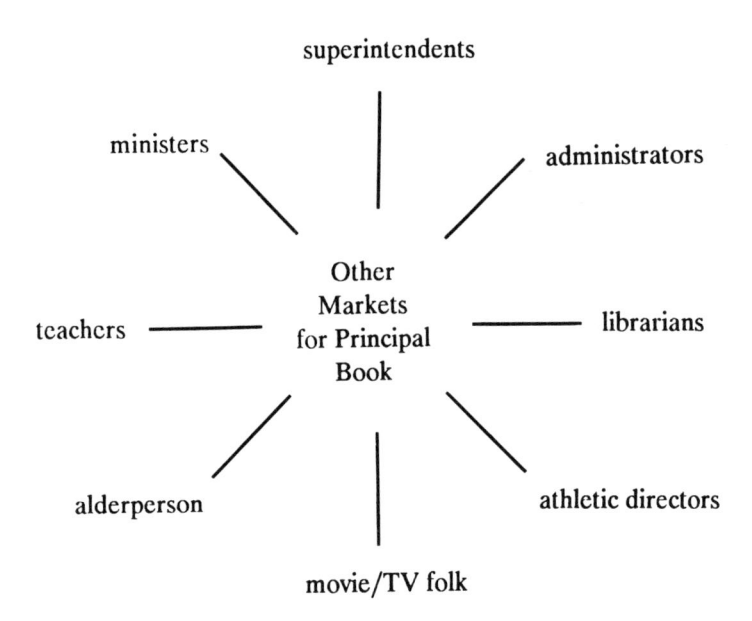

```
                    superintendents
                          |
    ministers             |            administrators
         \                |              /
          \               |             /
                  Other
                 Markets
    teachers ——  for Principal  —— librarians
                   Book
          /               |             \
         /                |              \
    alderperson           |            athletic directors
                          |
                    movie/TV folk
```

And what might the chapters of this new book contain or be about?

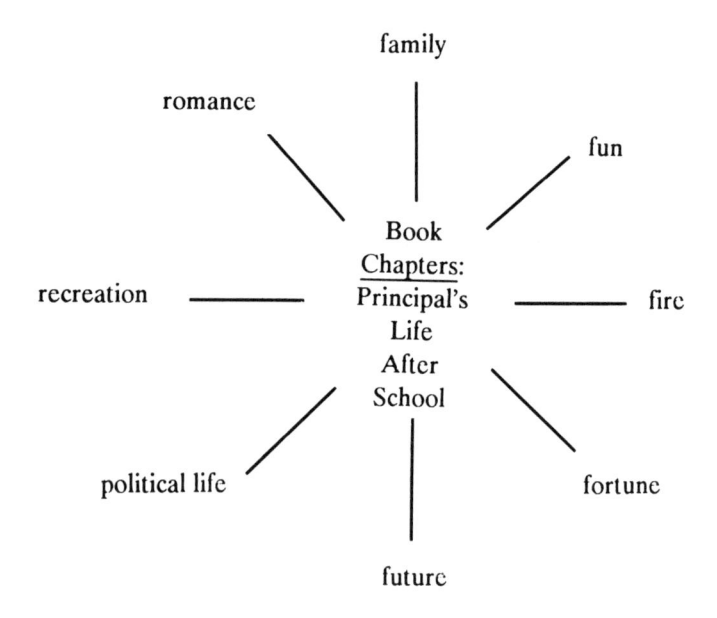

```
                       family
                          |
         romance           |
             \            |            fun
              \           |            /
                         Book
                       Chapters:
    recreation ——  Principal's  —— fire
                         Life
                        After
                        School
              /           |            \
             /            |             \
      political life      |            fortune
                          |
                       future
```

76   *Self-Publishing to*

And, finally, what other facets of principals' lives might I draw attention to in creating a book showing how they can expand their own activities and sense of fulfillment?

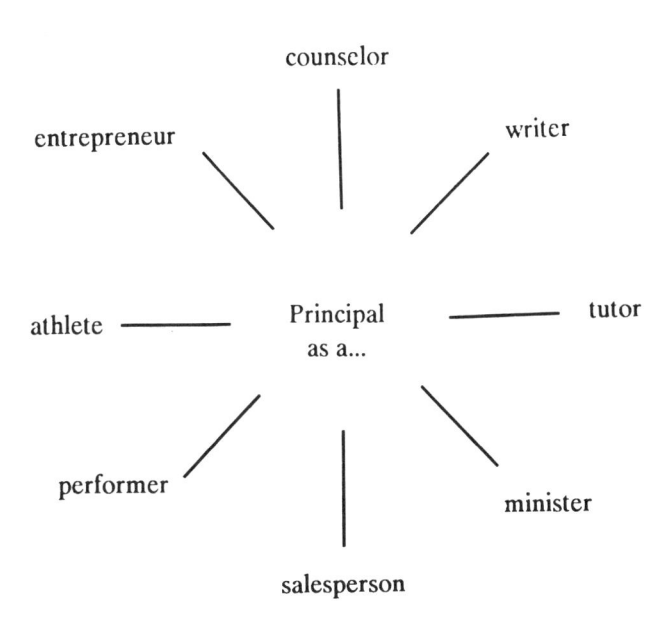

```
                    counselor
    entrepreneur        |         writer
              \         |        /
               \        |       /
                \       |      /
    athlete ——————  Principal  —————— tutor
                /     as a...   \
               /        |        \
              /         |         \
    performer           |          minister
                    salesperson
```

A closer look at the most appropriate non-book means

Let's look more closely at each of the preferred non-book means in terms of sharing our information with principals.

Rank of appropriateness:

(1.) **Talks/speeches**. Principals attend meetings; meetings often include talks and speeches. (Incidentally, the difference in the trade is that talks are given free, speeches mean payment to the speaker.) If an educational group will book the topic at a local gathering, regional meeting, or convention, you would have an interested and captive audience, particularly if the examples were tailored to the listeners and ample humor was injected. Could be done before or after the book appears, to plug it gently. Sometimes products are sold after presentations. If so, what better than to inflame listeners in the speech, then sell them the very book!

(2.) **Articles.** Written means are highly appropriate for academics, particularly articles. Best written and released at one of two times: (a) as the book is being written, to get in print near the date of the book's release to plug it in the author bio information: title, cost, how it can be obtained, and (2) after the book is in print, with contents tailored to the magazine's need, or with spinoff material learned after the book is written. This is a second chance to plug the book. The articles should be in magazines or journals read specifically by principals. Later, after each article is in print, you can reprint it (or excerpts from it) in the flyer sent to promote the book.

(3.) **Column.** Excellent if you can arrange with a publication that is widely read by principals to write a regular (or even occasional) column about the general topic of your book. Super visibility. Can't simply repeat what's in the book — in fact, can't do it at all. Build from it. Provide examples of the key points plus new information. Must include in your bio blurb the name of the book, cost, and how it can be obtained.

(4.) **Seminars/workshops.** If the subject concerned teachers, it would be ideal for in-house or in-district one-day programs. It might still work for principals and perhaps superintendents in larger districts, by combining districts, or at conventions. A workshop is an excellent follow-up to a speech and an ideal location at which to sell the book.

(5.) **Reports: pamphlets or brochures.** These might be written and printed later, about chapter length. They could be used to promote the book or they could be monthly subscription items. Their contents could expand upon the book's chapters or be about other topics related to principalship. When many of these have been written they could be anthologized or rewritten into a second book!

(6.) **Newsletter.** Best to produce after the book is published since the book buyers would be prime candidates for subscription. Would have to be jam-packed with information, how-to items, examples, etc. Extremely labor-intensive and financially risky. Better if two or three newsletters are done at once, a second perhaps about the principal/school or to superintendents about their extra-educational life. Build from already convinced clientele.

(7.) **Consulting**. Possible, but would an individual principal pay? It would be far better for consulting if the topic were school-related and the school pays.

Is somebody else already sharing this information by these means?

Research here takes time. I check the sources listed earlier for each category to see if others have written articles, columns, reports, or a newsletter. I see if anybody has spoken on the subject or is offering seminars or workshops. And I find absolutely no mention of it anywhere. Which means that if there's competition out there, it's local and well hidden.

That's the good news. .

The bad news: if this is such a hot topic am I the only genius around who sees it? Have a thousand tried it only to discover, through financial ruin and disgrace, that principals hate hearing about their non-school life and they shout anybody mentioning it off the stage and throw textbooks? I'll keep that in mind as I plod ahead, and think much harder about it before I invest much money.

Do I need purpose statements and all the rest?

Just because the field is empty doesn't mean I don't need a game plan!

The answer is yes, I need a purpose statement for every means, book or other method. The working question comes from that game plan, and the secondary questions flow from and help define the working question.

Since the process has already been explained, I won't develop the many purpose statements and the rest here. The process is identical to that for the book.

Is there sufficient material to develop each of these means?

Not now. This is a new field that, from what I can discover, nobody else has developed. So I will have to create a fresh body of information and, from that, spread it over a book and other means.

Yet if I can write a book about the topic I should easily be able to do most of the other things I envision in this chapter. If I had doubt I would look in depth now before wasting time on that means later. But I haven't any real doubt.

How will I integrate my other means?

I will give talks to any group of principals I can find beginning as soon as I have the bulk of the book researched, getting in lieu of money a list of names and addresses of all in attendance. (If they also offer money, I'll take it too!) Later I'll send a special letter and flyer to the listeners.

About the time I give the talks articles will be written about some aspect of the book, plugging its pending publication. Later, after the book is inprint, I'll continue writing articles with the book as the focus.

Once I've established contact with a publication for principals and it has run an article or two, I will approach the editor about a column, sending five or six examples with my query letter. Again, I'll include a plug for the book in the bio blurb with each column.

Once the book is out I will try to get scheduled at the larger gatherings of principals and superintendents, hoping to get paid and also to sell the book back-of-the-room. If not, I'll work in a handout with the talk that tells how to buy the book. I'll also convert this information into seminar or workshop form, seeing if I can follow a speech with a workshop later. These are best showcased at larger conventions so those who are impressed will book me in their districts.

Of course, once the book is in print I'll sell it when I can or at least get names and addresses and send follow-up promotion by mail since these are the very best buying prospects.

Finally, I'll look into the financial feasibility of creating reports of various related aspects, plus the wisdom of developing and offering a newsletter. These must wait until I see the interest the subject generates and the time and energy I have to put into both ventures.

A last, nagging suspicion: this subject isn't going to double my book money by the other means. Which means two things: (1) I should put proportionately less time into them and more into the book, and (2) I must make dead certain the book is going to sell well before I plan to earn from its spinoffs.

8 DETERMINING WHERE AND HOW TO SELL THE BOOK TO THE TARGETED MARKET

Once you have selected your market and have identified a particular market need to meet through your book, you must then determine where those in that market will buy your book. That, in turn, will help establish what the book must look like, what it should contain, and the tools you must develop to create sales.

Where do people usually buy books?

(1) at bookstores
(2) at home or work, by mail
(3) at gatherings such as conventions or conferences
(4) at seminars, workshops, talks, or speeches
(5) at stores other than bookstores
(6) at public stalls or booths
(7) at garage or library sales
(8) at or through a school, generally for a class
(9) at or through a business
(10) at their door

To reach a sizable percentage of your targeted market, selling at some of the ten locations will be ineffective. (1) Bookstores, unless they are specific stores with a certain clientele seeking particular kinds of books, are far too general or imprecise to reach many of your identified market. Other stores, (5), suffer from that same imprecision. Both (6) and (7) are rarely found and deal in a small quantity of diverse products, and (10), door-to-door selling, is atypical in the book market, even if the salesperson knew which doors belonged to your target market.

That leaves (2) by mail, (3) at gatherings such as conventions or conferences, (4) at seminars, workshops, talks, or speeches, (8) at or through a school, generally for a class, and (9) at or through a business.

Selling your book by mail

In most cases, selling your book by mail will probably be the most lucrative method, since TCE books are created for people who appear on accessible mailing lists and the potential buyers are, most likely, widely scattered and unaccustomed to finding or buying tightly-focussed books at a bookstore.

Selling by mail means two things: (1) the book's cover needn't attract attention nor will its appearance influence the sale since the actual book won't be seen until after it is ordered, and (2) the promotional tool sent by mail to sell the book is extraordinarily important.

A second form of mail sales can also be quite profitable: other groups (usually publishers) with book clubs that they promote by mail. To participate you must get your book accepted by that club, often selling it to them at production cost plus 10% of the sale cost to their members. Let's say that you sell your book for $15 and it costs you $1.80 to produce. And that they will sell your book to their members for $12. You would receive the $1.80 plus 10% of the $12 sales cost, or a total of $3 for every copy sold to the book club, which would pay the shipping and for all promotion.

Since book clubs normally buy when the book is new, preferring to keep the production costs low by increasing the number of books run at the first printing, that can bring you quick, early cash. But it can also reduce your number of direct buyers if the book club is working your targeted market. The ideal situation is where you sell directly to your targeted market and the book club works a wider, related field that would also benefit from reading your book.

There is a third potential market using mail in its selling: mail order firms which will purchase the book from you, either in bulk or through dropship. The same care must be taken to preserve the core of the targeted market for your own sales while using mail order groups to pick up secondary sales that you might otherwise miss.

Selling your book at gatherings

Selling a TCE book at gatherings like conventions or conferences can work well if

(1) your targeted market has such gatherings,
(2) many (preferably most or all) of the members attend them,
(3) the attendance totals of each are fairly large,
(4) the number of such gatherings isn't excessive or they aren't too widely scattered,
(5) there is a means of selling books at the gatherings in a well publicized or much frequented area, and
(6) book purchases are encouraged.

This form of book selling would be even more effective if the participants were already aware of the book through an earlier mailing and if you spoke at the gathering and drew attention to the book's availability.

Selling your book at presentations

Seminars, workshops, talks, and speeches can be excellent ways both to make listeners aware of your book and to offer it immediately. What you say and how well you say it can have considerable impact on the book's sale. Buyers want more good things from an articulate, organized, informed source, and if your presentation shows you to be all of that, many sales should follow.

A request or permission to offer a seminar/workshop or a talk or speech usually comes because you have demonstrated your expertise through a book, which an organization often first hears about through a flyer you send in the mail. This then becomes a highly effective means of follow-up penetration which, in turn, sells more books and, through the program, further validates your expertise.

Selling your book for class or educational use

Teachers can be extremely effective in selling books. The very best kind of TCE book to sell this way would be one containing information necessary to receive a license or certification. If it were the only book with that information, it would be mandatory reading of every teacher, plus every student seeking that kind of validation.

Many books aren't that fortunate, but they can come close. Other than being the only book about the topic, a book can be the only one to approach the subject in a certain way. Or its strength can come from its clarity of explanation or its inclusion of new information not found elsewhere. Or the way it uses charts or illustrations or worksheets to convert the text to practical application.

Whatever unique quality your book has (and why would you publish a book if it weren't somehow unique?), that distinction must be brought to the teachers' attention. Free copies may have to be provided so teachers can review the text before adopting it. Which probably means mailing brochures first, plus some groundswell promotion through reviews, information in association publications, and so on.

Selling books for class or some educational use sometimes produces few initial sales but rather a steady and growing long-term income base from new learners entering the field.

Selling your book at or through businesses

Businesses can be quite influential in purchasing and promoting a TCE book. If the book meets a specific need of a business's employees, it will likely buy as many copies as it has employees who will benefit.

If the book helps a client or customer better understand, use, or desire a product or service offered by that business, it may well buy your book in large volume to sell or give to customers. Or it may negotiate with you to produce a modified version of your book to be used as a premium giveaway.

If your targeted market works for just one or a few firms or most or all are affected by what a key firm does or says, that can have a huge influence on your book's sale and where it is bought. I.B.M. is an easy example of the latter. Whether friend, foe, or curious observer, computerfolk cannot ignore I.B.M.'s action — or inaction. If your book uniquely addresses an I.B.M. product or service, it too cannot be ignored.

So if the needs of a business and the contents of your book overlap, your making your book's message and its availability known to that business can boost sales mightily. The degree to which this might affect the specific content of the book — the illustrations or in-house terminology used, for example — is directly related to the influence the business in question has on the targeted market or the quantity of books they will buy. If that's large enough, prepare an edition exclusively for that firm.

Your task now

First you must identify where your targeted market would buy your book, then list those locations in the order of likelihood. In the next chapter we will see what we must promise them to get them to make that purchase — and how we will make them aware of those promises.

EXAMPLE

Where Would the Principals Buy My Book?

Let's go through all ten choices, to eliminate some, select others, and put the winners in order.

(1) **Bookstore**. No, principals wouldn't expect to find any book specifically about their jobs or personal needs in a bookstore. If they did, they might not buy it because it is in the bookstore! The long shot would be that their spouses might see the book there and buy it for them.

(2) **By mail**. Yes, they would probably buy in response to a flyer sent directly to them at school, though if I could get their home addresses, they might give the flyer more attention if it were received outside the office.

(3) **At gatherings** such as conventions or conferences. Yes, they would likely pick up a flyer and may read it later. A booth selling the book would attract many passersby. All the more effective if I spoke at the gathering and called attention to the book's availability at a booth.

(4) **At seminars, workshops, talks, or speeches.** Yes, but there wouldn't be too many such opportunities, and some of the academic sponsors would balk at selling in these situations.

(5) **At stores other than bookstores.** No, for the same reason they wouldn't usually seek or buy this book at a bookstore. Unless it was a store specifically for educators or principals — or, again, the book were bought by a spouse.

(6) **At public stalls or booths.** No.

(7) **At garage or library sales.** No.

(8) **At or through a school,** generally for a class. It's possible that after the book had been out and accepted by principals, it could be worked into the reading of an education class for administrators. But not probable since its scope lies well beyond most such classes.

(9) **At or through a business.** No.

(10) **At their door.** A sane salesperson selling exclusively at the doors of principals? No.

How would I rank those with affirmative replies?

A principal would be most likely to buy this book by mail in response to a flyer I sent the same way.

After that, at gatherings. Twice as likely after I had mailed the flyer, these people were aware of the book's existence, were curious about its contents and appearance, and — all the better — I had spoken to them. The word-of-mouth factor could play a huge role here. If the fliers had been sent and some or many of the principals in attendance had already bought the book, when they gathered with peers and the book was visible or mentioned, those favorably impressed would give valuable, unsolicited testimonials to those around them, which, in turn, would stimulate a rush of sales.

The same thing would be true of offering the book after a seminar, workshop, talk, or speech. If the participants already knew about the book through fliers and that, in part, had sparked their interest in attending the presentation, unless I did something to dampen or kill their interest, I could expect virtually every participant to buy a copy.

The least likely way would be as a text or recommended reading for a class. If that were to happen, it would be because the book was already popular and accepted.

9 IDENTIFYING THE PROMISES THE BOOK'S PROMOTION MUST MAKE AND WHAT THE PROMOTIONAL TOOL MUST INCLUDE

Actually, more important than where your book will be bought is why it will be bought at all. Why your targeted market will reach into their pockets, pull out money, and buy a book knowing that they will still have to plow through hundreds of pages of prose before they reap an ounce of reward.

Your first foe is inertia. It's far easier to do nothing than something. Not to buy a book and not to read it, doing something else or nothing instead, is far more alluring. So you must overwhelm inertia.

Your second foe is inaction. Inertia means remaining in a fixed condition without change. Inaction is the absence of action. They sound almost the same yet the difference, in terms of your profit, is that which separates poverty from wealth. But buyers recognize that they should do something, should buy your book, read it, and reap the rewards. But they don't. They make a decision not to act.

One way to break the holds of inertia and inaction is to convince potential buyers that the rewards from buying your book and applying its contents can be so great, and so desirable, that only a fool would not do so.

You must make promises, or at least dangle lures, so bright, so convincing, and so desirable that the price and the effort to get the book are insignificant in comparison to what it will or can bring.

There's a catch: what you promise or dangle must be true!

It is how you frame the truth and how you get people them to read it that we are discussing here: the promises the promotion must make and the kind of tool, and its contents, needed to get those promises before your potential buyers' eyes.

An antidote to inertia and inaction?

There is no universal cure to either lamentable condition. In TCE publishing, though, there's one remedy that almost always works: find a need desperately felt by your targeted market, then show through your book how that need can be met.

The greater the desperation or the larger the number in your targeted market who want to meet the need, the greater your book's selling potential. As important, you must highlight the benefits or rewards they can expect from meeting that need. And somewhere prominent in the promotional text they must be told in terms they can understand and apply that the book explains precisely what they need to know.

You have already identified your target market's need. Now you must focus on what gets buyers to make the purchase: the benefits.

Identifying the benefits

Ask yourself: what rewards might your book buyer reasonably expect if he/she could fully satisfy that market need? Asking some additional questions might help:

(1) Why does the person have that need?
(2) When?
(3) Where?
(4) Who else has that need in addition to those in the target market?

Then list every reward, every positive and desired benefit that comes to mind for helping a person solve the need in each situation. Obvious benefits are love, joy, happiness, fulfillment. TCE benefits also include more income, greater prestige, a competitive edge, less toil, promotion, security.

Put the benefits one could expect from meeting that need in a priority order as valued by your target market. Ask which benefits would be sought the most by the greatest number of your target market. List every benefit from the most likely to the least.

Some benefits simply can't be provided by a book or by a book alone: they stretch beyond the reach of the written word and what it can do. But sometimes a book can tell all. So at this point you must determine which of those benefits, from the top of the list moving down, your book can bring its buyer, if applied as written. (If later research shows your list is too optimistic, you can delete the benefits that can't be met before you produce the final promotional tool.)

The benefits that remain are the promises your promotional tool must make. The tool exists primarily to tell why the buyer needs to or would want to buy your book. Why? To receive those benefits or rewards!

the rigorous scrutiny of acceptable research. But it has one function only, to meet a specific need. And through how the book meets that need, promises can be made to those who apply its contents, promises that will be modified in the final promotional tool as necessary.

A quick review of where we are and how we got here

Sometimes it is refreshing and enlightening to put what we've shared into a capsulated perspective, to show in a slightly different way what this chapter is about. Three steps of a quick review:

(1) Much of the success of the TCE approach comes from the clarity with which you identify (a) your target market, (b) the needs it will pay to meet by book and other information dissemination means, and (c) the ways by which you make that market aware of those needs and your ability to meet them.

(2) Your promotional tool(s) must (a) tell potential buyers of your book that they have a need and what it is, (b) how they would benefit from meeting that need, (c) how your book will help them do that, and (d) why they should buy your book now.

(3) To do that you (a) must identify the specific target market most likely to buy your book, (b) customize that book's content to meet a key need of that specific target market, (c) provide actual and obvious help to meet that need in your book, and (d) let all potential buyers of your book know that the book that can help meet their need is available, why it should be bought, and where and how it can be obtained.

How can you tell potential buyers to buy your book?

There may be 100 different ways, but most buyers become aware of books by:

(1) a flyer or brochure in the mail
(2) a space or classified ad in a magazine, journal, newspaper, newsletter, etc.
(3) a display in a bookstore, at a convention or seminar, etc.
(4) a review in a publication

Tightly-Targeted Markets

Said in a different way, what you tell the potential buyer creates a set of expectations. You say that the book can solve a problem or meet a need. That the buyer can expect certain rewards from that resolution. And that your book contains what they need to know.

Your promotional tool creates expectations which your book must meet.

All of those promises, all of the expectations, dictate what your final promotional tool must include. Plus the necessary information about how the book can be ordered or bought, its cost, when it can be expected, what qualifies you to write it, and whatever must be explained about its content to convince the buyer that it will do what you promise.

The promotional tool is your blueprint for action

The beauty of designing a promotional tool as you are creating a book is the singlemindedness of its intent and the focus it provides for research and writing.

Earlier you wrote a purpose statement, converted it into a working question, and from that produced a general ideological framework for your book. Secondary questions gave it a rough outline. Now you are asking why those in your targeted market would want to buy this information. What benefits would they receive? From this you are creating a rough promotional tool.

Later you will conduct the actual research and write the book. Your rough outline will take final form, probably with alterations and some redirection. Some of the original promises proposed to the buyer may be less clear; new promises may emerge. So you may have to adjust the final promotional tool some.

Why you develop an initial promotional tool now is to provide guidance to help determine the particular avenues of inquiry you must pursue to make the book valuable and marketable. By tentatively identifying the selling promises now, you are narrowing the range of unnecessary information at the research and writing stage.

The promotional tool gives you a standard against which you can ask: does that information fulfill the book's promises?

Which does not mean that the truth is in any way compromised or that the only facts that are admitted are those which support the book's predetermined theme. It means that the book is written for a very specific purpose to an identified target market, and that everything included meets

(5) a review on radio or TV
(6) referral in an article or book — any form of print media
(7) referral on radio or TV — any form of other media
(8) referral by the author in a speech, seminar, etc.
(9) personal referral from another person
(10) use as a textbook or required or suggested reading
(11) an actual copy in a library, bookstore, or other location
(12) a news release or conference about the book or author
(13) an award for the book or author
(14) a booklist
(15) a book club
(16) a card deck received in the mail
(17) a catalog
(18) telephone solicitation

In the previous chapter it was determined that TCE books would most likely be sold five ways: by mail, at gatherings, at oral presentations, for a class, or at or through a business. The book would either be sold by a flyer or on display, though the latter would be enhanced by informing the targeted market by mail of the book's existence and purpose.

Therefore, our focus here is on a flyer (or brochure).

What must your flyer do?

Why are you promoting your book? Because you want to sell it to at least 10% of your targeted market, which by conventional direct mail standards is exceptionally high. Therefore, to reach this goal your flyer must convince its recipient that

(1) he or she has a pressing need or problem;
(2) your book offers an (immediately) applicable solution;
(3) it is the only way that solution can be obtained, or it is the best solution available;
(4) meeting the need or solving the problem is far more valuable than the cost of the book;
(5) your credentials or expertise give you the authority to offer this solution;
(6) the solution is fully and professionally explained, and
(7) your book should be bought now!

Even more, the flyer must do these four things:

(1) reach the decisionmaker's hands;
(2) inform, convince, sell;
(3) make the ordering process quick and simple, and
(4) look as good or better than the book itself.

To do those things, what must it contain? A detailed study of other, excellent book-selling fliers is in order, particularly those sent to your target market. What is the competition? What are they circulating? What must you include? What can you do better?

I can only give a general reply here, based on a review of a wide variety of such fliers. Most include the following:

(1) a headline featuring a benefit or need
(2) the book's title prominently displayed
(3) copy telling why the book should be bought
(4) the book's cost
(5) how the book is bound
(6) testimonials about the book and/or author
(7) references (sometimes testimonials too) about earlier, related books by the author
(8) excerpts from the book
(9) an illustration or photo of the book itself
(10) a photo of the author
(11) biographical information about the author emphasizing qualifications related to the book being promoted
(12) a table of contents
(13) an order form with an address, credit card fill-in instructions, to whom a check should be written, shipping costs, tax information, lines for the buyer's address and ZIP, and sometimes a number for credit card orders by phone
(14) sometimes a return envelope, sometimes with prepaid postage

How much of the flyer must you prepare now?

You must know the promises you will make and the expectations you will create to get your book bought. They should be written out at this stage, word-by-word, precisely and clearly. (You can modify them later.)

That is no simple task. It provides the spine and direction of your research and writing. It is very important. You must know while you research, write, and produce the book what its buyers will expect to see on its pages. The hooks you will emphasize to induce them to buy. The particular benefits they can expect from their purchase, the guidelines and how-to information and processes, and so on, that you have promised to include in your book to help them meet a need.

That's it. No preliminary drawings, no ad copy or typesetting. Later, when the artwork for the book's cover exists, when you know how long the book will be, when you know how many of the original promises can be made and kept, when you have a good photo of yourself, and when 100 more details can be answered, then it is time for the selling tool(s) to be sculpted.

Identify the heart now. Build the body later.

EXAMPLE

Since I expect that most principals will buy my book in response to a flyer that I'll send them by mail, I must now figure out what I should put on that flyer to make them jump at the chance to buy my tome!

A small diagram helps me see ways to prepare the best possible promotional tool:

NEED	**BUYER**
Whole life beyond school	Principals

My book must help principals lead a fuller, better life beyond school. The flyer must show that that is what my book does — or their money back. Plus why they'd want a whole — fuller, better — life beyond school, and what that means.

Tightly-Targeted Markets

So here I identify and put into words what goes on that crucial flyer: raw material from which promises will be made about the book to get the buyers' attention.

Later I will worry about the flyer's actual preparation, and the size, type style, paper texture, illustrations, etc.

What I must know now are the needs that the book will meet and the benefits it will bring. Without knowing those I don't know why a person would buy my book. Conversely, by knowing them they become the selling components of my promotional flyer. It'd be useful to know who else has similar needs. Then I should zero in on the most wanted of those benefits and put that list in some priority order. A look again at the purpose statement will see if I'm still on track. Then I have to reduce those key promises to their final, pulling words. Words that will get order forms filled and payment eagerly sent!

Needs that this book meets

If I wrote a book about creating a fuller, better life for principals beyond school what would that book talk about? In no particular order, it might show how to

(1) establish a better balanced life
(2) put the job/position into proper perspective
(3) develop other talents/skills outside of the school setting
(4) direct the principal's personal growth to qualify him/her for a subsequent job, or to be able to enjoy a desired avocation
(5) invest money wisely, to give the principal maximum flexibility later
(6) identify and develop other income sources while principal
(7) build on-going, effective avenues of communication with one's spouse and children
(8) learn to best utilize the "goldfish bowl" reality of being principal
(9) establish/maintain a wholesome exercise regimen

Needs converted into benefits

Meeting needs is one thing. But converting those needs into benefits is what will get me buyers. What rewards will the principals get from reading my book and doing what it says?

(1) less stress
(2) fuller creative growth
(3) financial security and/or sense of control
(4) optimum physical or emotional health
(5) positive family relationship
(6) sense of control over the future
(7) less dependence upon the job for financial or emotional fulfillment
(8) healthy, effective distance from the role, thus clearer evaluation and decisionmaking
(9) new vigor for life

Who else has similar needs?

While I'm at it, it makes sense to begin a list of other vocations that have similar needs. Some might buy this book. I might expand the target to include principals and other groups. Or I might use the format I develop in this book and produce another, similar book for another group. At the outset it seems that superintendents, athletic directors, other administrators in the educational field, and many other administrators in general would have similar needs. I can further define, and expand upon, this list while I'm researching and writing the book.

Putting those benefits in an order

Some benefits or rewards are more appealing than others. Finding the right benefit is like finding the right tree: it can yield bountifully forever! Which is precisely what I have in mind for my book.

So I will select from the benefits I've identified those that I think will appeal most to principals and create my promises from them.

Must this be guesswork? Not at all. I could test it three ways. One, I could make a list of benefits or promises and simply ask principals, "If there were (five) books and from buying each you would get one of these benefits, would you buy first?" "Second?" "Third?"

Or I could ask advertising folk who sell to buyers in the same socio-economic level as principals what makes those people buy? What do they want?

Which benefits are most likely to get them to buy a book?

Or I could test different fliers, each headlining a different benefit, to see which sells the best.

But for now I am guessing. Along the way, though, since I'm gambling with my money I will indeed ask the principals, and if I find a salesperson who looks knowledgeable about this group of buyers I will ask him or her, and I might well test various fliers too. But I must start somewhere.

My sense is that principals, once they have spent a few years learning the role, grow antsy. They are about as high in the structure as they will or want to go. Their pay is adequate but won't increase much. The stress and burnout level is high. Being the principal affects their activities in the community, their children ("that's because your dad [or mom] is the principal!"), and their spouses. And their vocational future beyond principalship is dim.

Based on that, by focussing on which benefits would I most likely be able to get them to buy my book?

(1) Building now for a fuller, richer life during and after principalship
(2) Putting more money in their pockets
(3) Getting their life in control and balance
(4) Bringing new vigor to their life

Or by some combination of these benefits.

Are those consistent with our purpose statement?

A look at the purpose statement again

The purpose statement says "The purpose of this book is to share with principals ways by which they can serve their schools, families, and communities with love and lasting distinction while also leading balanced, challenging, full lives during and after their principalship."

All four fall easily within the broader purpose statement, with one reminder: the service to school would be a largely undeveloped segment of my book, with the understanding that by making a principal more vigorous, more secure, or more fulfilled the school would also benefit. Also, the emphasis on service to the school, family, and community is related to the academic role of principal. I would stress other service, as a fuller person in a community and in the home.

For now, nothing inconsistent. For later, I may have to tighten up considerably on that purpose statement.

Some promises and expectations that will sell my book!

I prefer to state these more as headlines or questions, assuming that the book buyer will consider them promises that the book will fulfill or expectations of what the book will do. And I prefer to bunch them together, thinking that if each of the benefits has a certain appeal, many together would have more appeal. The only danger is promising so much that you go beyond credibility.

Here are some starters, which I will add to when I title the book two chapters hence:

"You won't be a principal forever. Let us help you build a fuller, richer life now for a brighter, more prosperous future later."

"Is the 'out-of-school' you building a better, balanced, brighter future?"

"Principals: are you creating a better you while you create a better school?"

"Principals: find your family, fun, fire, fortune, and a bright future while you keep the building intact and the teachers awake!"

10 EVALUATING POTENTIAL PROFIT AGAINST WORKING CAPITAL

To this point you have been forming a book from the rough clay of ideas and hope, to mold it into some early, recognizable form. Yet books are major investments to create and publish. They cost in time, energy, and plain old cash.

Energy is a given at each step. I have tried to reduce the time investment at the planning stages to the minimum, aware that every idea doesn't result in a book. In fact, most drop out by now, so keeping the time investment small gives you more time to pursue other, stronger ideas or other, non-book ventures.

Here the third element, cash, becomes a factor, before you harden that clay into its final form. The questions are simple: how much will it cost? Do you have, or can you get, enough capital to finance the book? And will the profit earned be worth the time, energy, and money spent?

We need some starting numbers to make evaluative decisions. So let's revert to an earlier goal — $50,000 profit from the book — and move backward from there, plugging in, for the sake of calculation, some cost figures I have derived from years as a publisher.

The cost of earning a $50,000 profit from your book

A standard publisher would have to sell 24,723 books at $15@ to pay you $50,000 in royalties at today's conventional royalty rates. How many books would you need to write, self-publish, and sell to reap the same income?

Again, some basic facts: you want $50,000 profit from a $15 book. Say it costs you 50% of that $15 to produce and promote your book and that by using the TCE approach you intend to sell to 10% of your targeted market.

Thus $15 divided by 2 = $ 7.50 profit per book. That means it will cost you $50,000 to earn $50,000 in profit; said another way, the book must gross $100,000 in sales. To gross $100,000 you must sell 6,667 books. About 27%

of what the standard publisher must sell. Using the 10% ratio, your target market would need 66,670 potential buyers. If a standard publisher used the same ratio, their market would need 247,230 potential buyers.

Let's use rough calculations to see when you would need your $50,000.

Initial book production costs: $16,500

You would need the initial book production costs first:

Research	$ 1,400
Overhead	500
Electronic typesetting	1,000
Cover preparation	1,000
Illustrations	1,000
Printing (6800 books)	10,200
Shipping	900
	$ 16,000

Some of the numbers require a brief explanation. First, I have no idea if you need to spend any money for research. You might already know everything anyone would want to read about your subject, in which case this money stays in your pocket. The same with overhead: you may be using the company computer during lunchtime and hand delivering the mail. So adjust these numbers accordingly. You'll likely need some funds for both, though.

There are three ways to get type set inexpensively at the level needed for a commercial book: straight from the computer, proportionally printed; from the computer through a laser printer, or from the computer, coded, to a more advanced electronic phototypesetter. While laser printers are getting better and less expensive, the third system is my preference here, figured at about $6 a running foot of copy. A quick calculation will see that I am thinking of a book of 200 pages or a bit longer: a first nonfiction text mercifully lean and gracefully direct.

It is no facile cliche that a book is judged (and bought) by its cover. So you spend to have a cover professionally designed and prepared for the printer. Yet in the TCE mode you will sell mostly by mail and the book will more likely be bought because it meets a dire need. Thus your cover needn't be as flashy; on the other hand, it must photograph clearly and look sharp. The demands are different but the cost won't be far less. $1,000 should easily cover the cover.

Tightly-Targeted Markets

Illustrations are the great unknown. If you use charts and simple, computer-aided graphics, $1,000 will be far too much. If you use intricate artwork drawn by a professional, it may not be enough. Again, adjust accordingly.

Printing the book may run you 10% of its ultimate cost — more if the illustrations need to be in colors other than black and white. And much more if you produce very small quantities. (It will cost at least twice as much per book to print 500 copies as it will 5,000.) I'm presuming about 200 pages, all b/w but the cover, which will be a trade paperback. For 6,800 copies it may cost $10,200, at $1.50 each.

Shipping is also an unknown. Usually your best bids will be printed somewhere across the country, which means you must pay to get the books to your warehouse. $900 is my calculation, again to be adjusted to your reality.

Promotional costs: $26,750

Next you will need promotional funds. The artwork must come first, of course. The rest will be spent to prepare and mail fliers to the targeted market:

Flyer art preparation	$ 1,500
Print/mail at $ .37875@ to 66,670	25,250
	$ 26,750

The flyer you will send to your targeted market is the single most important selling tool you will create. So put its creation in the hands of professionals who turn out quality products: an ad agency with graphics capacity. Shop around and make certain that the flyer says what it must to appeal to your buyers. $1,500 should be plenty.

A well conceived flyer is no better than its appearance in final, printed form. Make certain that the printer produces a mailer worth that initial investment and the huge postage costs that follow. That is, bid printers carefully, see what they have produced, and get your costs and deadlines clear and firm. Then contact a mailing house to send the fliers to your mailing list by bulk rate. The consensus of my direct mailing colleagues is that in early 1989 you should be able to get a classy item to your market for pennies less than the $ .37875@ budgeted.

Fulfillment and tax/postage reserve fund: $7,250

State tax and postage should be paid by the buyer, although a contingency fund must be set aside for those who don't include the money in their order. (It's easier to pay it than try to get it from these losers, frankly.)

Then when they order you must package and ship the book their way. That's called fulfillment, and whether you do this yourself or you farm it out to someone else, figure it will cost you about $1 an order, which we will calculate high here at $1 a book.

Tax/postage reserve fund	$ 583
Fulfillment	6,667
	$ 7,250

Do you have, or can you get, enough capital to finance the book?

Hardly anybody has an extra $50,000 sitting around waiting for a book to be written. No bank will ante up that kind of moola for an amateur with a book in mind, without a big house or a fleet of new cars to back it up. Even investment brokers aren't that balmy.

You'll have to have the money yourself, get it from a relative or literary angel (with an 800 number in heaven), go into hock, or find some other source. Sobering possibilities.

But don't despair. You can get by for about $10,000. It's just much, much faster — and the return is that much quicker — the more you can invest at the outset.

You see, you don't need all $50,000 on the first day. You can invest the profits you make as the book sells to generate money to cover later expenses. Let's follow three scenarios, leaving you to imagine a hundred deviations in between.

The fat cat approach: money when you need it!

Here you have the initial $16,000 for book production and the costs as estimated are about right. You have the book electronically phototypeset, a fine looking cover produced, and 6,800 copies of the book printed.

You can afford the flyer art preparation, its printing, and the full mailing to all 66,670 lucky recipients. Another $26,750— or $42,750.

The rest you can pull from profits. The tax/postage fund and the fulfillment costs can be paid from the $100,000 you are going to get back. In short, even financial fat cats need only $42,750 to make $100,000 gross.

The skinny cat approach: about half the money you need

If you've got $25,000, the first $16,000 is going to cover the initial book production costs, again assuming that estimates are about right. All 6,800 copies of the book are printed and the book is back in local storage, probably your garage or basement.

You know that you can earn that last $7,250 as the books come in, so that leaves $9,000 to invest in promotion. The first $1,500 goes to flyer art prep. Then $7,500 for flyer printing and mailing, which means you can print and mail exactly 19,802 fliers. At a 10% sale ratio, you can expect to earn $29,700, minus the $1,980 for fulfillment, or about $27,500, setting several hundred aside for the tax/postage fund. From the $27,500 you can afford 72,607 fliers, mailed— far more than the 46,868 buyers left in your field.

I would do that a bit differently, however. Rather than having just 19,802 fliers printed, I would arrange to have all 66,670 (or 66,700) printed, paying half in advance, half in 30 days, and mailing to all I can from my remaining $7,500. Within 30 days I will have earned from books sold far more than my debt to the printer, and as the books continue to sell I would continue to have the fliers mailed out, until the market is covered. That way I get the fliers done cheaper in bulk and I have them ready to mail the day my postage money is in hand.

The drawback for the skinny cat? Time. The quicker the fliers are out, the faster the profits return. So sending fliers out in two or several spurts simply delays the money coming back.

The other, modest disadvantage? The timing. If you plan to follow up or coordinate the book's release with other selling means, or a publicity campaign, it is hard to do so effectively with the items creeping into the market in successive mailings.

The alley cat approach: almost no money but plenty of time!

Here you are going to pick apart those initial book production costs. You will write a book with little or no research costs, or you will absorb them into your other living or job expenses. The same with overhead. And you'll try to design the book without costly illustrations.

Where you can't afford to scrimp is in the contents, appearance, and cover of the book. The typesetting must be at the level of other books your market buys, and the cover must be good and professional looking, so you can expect to pay the needed $2,000 for those, or less if quality is maintained. Shipping, too, is a variable you can't control much, though you could investigate the cost of leaving some of the printed books in storage at the printers for one or several months, seeing if storage and second shipping costs are reasonable while you sell books to cover later freight.

The major change would be in the number of books printed. Below 2,000 the per unit cost rises quickly, so my suggestion would be 2,000 books in the first printing, expecting to pay about $2.65 each (if you paid $1.50@ for 6,800). Added to the $2,900 already spent for typesetting, the cover, and shipping, that would increase your initial production costs to $8,200.

You have $1,800 left, plus a potential income of $30,000 from the sale of the 2,000 books. Your $1,800 isn't enough to make a dent in the direct mail market. So why not sell 1/3 of your 2,000 books other ways, to build a kitty of $10,000 to begin the direct mail campaign to your targeted market? You may need $1,000 of your remaining $1,800 to sell those 2,000 books, but as soon as you gather another $700 to add to the remaining $800 you could have the flyer art prepared. Then when you approach the $10,000, get the fliers printed and mailed. From there, you do much as the skinny cat did: every time you sell enough books, you send out more fliers! Except that when you run out of books you get another batch printed. Eventually you should sell all 6,667 books!

The greater cost of this slow and somewhat labyrinthian route? Less than $50,000 profit because the books, printed in lots of 2,000 or so, cost more per unit, which means less profit for you. (For example, if it costs $2.65 for the first and second printings of 2,000 each and $2.50 for the third of 2,800, your total book printing cost would be $17,600, or $7,400 more than had all 6,800 books been printed at $1.50.)

The second cost: the loss of the timing impact of mailing the fliers to all in your market at once, with the promotional, publicity, and follow-up advantages that could bring.

There's an obvious question left dangling: how are you going to sell that 1/3 of the 2,000 books, or 667, to create the direct mail kitty of $10,000?

Tightly-Targeted Markets

In Chapter 8 we asked where the targeted market would most likely buy your book. By mail was the preferred choice, but you haven't got the cash to take the "A" train, so let's look at other ways by which you can gather ticket money.

Six other paths were promising for TCE books: to book clubs, to other mail order firms dealing in similar books, at gatherings (probably conventions or conferences), at presentations (seminars, workshops, talks, and speeches), for class use, and to or through a business.

In Chapter 9 we mentioned 18 more ways that you can tell potential customers about your book. Some obvious ways might be pursued with the $1,000 at hand: getting the book reviewed in the publications that your targeted market reads, running a display ad in the same specialized publications, and even testing it for sale by telephone solicitation.

What you must do is think 667 books and a $1,000 expense fund, then devise the surest means to make those sales. But don't overlook the most obvious: talk directly to the 15 or 20 people you know best in that market and sell them. Move out from there. Talk to your local chapter, then the state, then the convention. Set up a booth. Comb the market to get others to sell your books, giving them the standard 40-50% discount if bought in lots of 10 or more. Talk to teachers who would benefit from using your book as a text. Talk directly to businesses, sell by phone. Do the things you would do after the direct mail solicitation if you were a fat, or even skinny, cat. Do it in reverse. Alley cats persevere.

Will the profit earned be worth the time, energy, and money spent?

Only you can answer that. We are calculating a 50% profit. For every dollar you put up, you get it plus another dollar back — quickly. Financially that should satisfy anyone.

As for energy, that's what gets the money doubled: you run the risk and put in the effort rather than letting a standard publisher do both and give you 15% or less. Is it worth your effort?

And time. If you write a book rather than earn a million dollars another way, and earnings are your criterion, then it isn't worth it. But if you write a book after hours or in your spare time and it means much more to you than the dollars alone, any profit is a boon.

To determine whether the profit is worth the time, calculate the hours it will take you to prepare, produce, and publish the book. Convert that into a dollar rate, so much per hour. Add that to the costs of the book. Subtract that from the gross income (or anticipated gross income) and what remains is profit. Then answer the question yourself: is it worth it?

EXAMPLE

Good news/bad news. The good news is that there are from 75,000-79,000 principals who can be reached by a mailing list. Let's say 75,000. If I sold a $15 book to 10%, I would receive $112,500. If my profit were 50% by selling by direct mail, I would reap $56,250. Sign me up!

But if that profit would cost me as much as I could earn, I would need to invest $56,250. Even subtracting the tax/postage reserve fund and the fulfillment costs ($583 and $7,500) of $8,083, I'd still need $48,167. Slow down!

So much for the fat cat/skinny cat route. I can scrape together a flat $14,000 by dipping as deep as I can go into every pocket. The entrepreneur's woe.

My task is simple: verify the numbers before I go a step further.

Initial book production costs

Research. Time to set some limits. In the next chapter I'll give the book its final form. Now I have to see if I can afford to do it at all. As for research, I should be able to find plenty of how-to information locally by interviewing several local principals, then make some phone calls to principals in other states, using their quotes to give the book a more nationwide appeal. Will I have to travel to get those quotes? How much will the phone bill increase? That's about it for research, other than paper and stamps and some driving around that I can absorb out of my pocket. I'll write down $750 now and hope to reduce that to maybe $200 if I don't have to travel.

Overhead. Phone and supplies are in the research money. I have a small computer, I'm already paying the house bills, and I'll write at home on weekends or at night. No new costs here. Saved $500! (Self-deception is my hyphenated middle name.)

Electronic phototypesetting. Well, the guy says there are three ways to make the book look good. The first is out: my software doesn't have proportional spacing, or if it does I don't know how to use it. And what I saw of that on other machines isn't how I want my book to look anyway.

Two calls to see how much a laser printer would cost: out of the question! I hear that they can be rented at quick print shops — but not around here. So that leaves electronic phototypesetting, whatever that is.

A check with Dan Poynter's *The Self-Publishing Manual*. He says I could draft and edit the text on my computer and send it by phone to a typesetter to get regular book (photo-composition) type. Or I could take my disk and they could produce the book copy that way. So I look under "Typesetting" in the "Yellow Pages" in the directory of a larger city nearby: 9 choices!

I call each and say I am thinking of self-publishing a 200-page book, have an "X" computer (CPM/"Y" software), and am interested in having the copy typeset either from my disk or by phone (through a modem). Do they have facilities for that and how much does it cost a running foot?

Three are vague or disinterested. The others tell me that yes, glad to help, why don't I stop by and they can give me exact quotes when they have more details. That means a day in the city: five are open on Saturday, so they are my targets.

The result: depending upon how much precoding I do and the kind of computer/software I have, plus whether I send it by modem or not, a wide range of prices. I boil that down to three who will set directly off my disk (saving me the cost of buying a modem), all charging about the same: one hour of consulting to set up a coding base for the heads, sub-titles, numbering, and text (from $50-65/hr) plus $5-6 a running foot of text, plus a one-time set-up fee of $10. Figure another $50 for text corrections for miscoding. Which means that if my book is 6" x 9" I will have about 7 1/4" of type per full page. Then a 200-page book will contain at most 1,450 running inches, or about 121 running feet. That times $6 is $726, plus $65, $10, and $50 = $851. Some pages will be shorter, like chapter endings and spots with art inserts; some text will be added later, like the index, with another set-up fee. These might offset each other. I'll keep the $1,000 in the budget and expect to save $100 of that.

Cover preparation. I want my cover to look good, period. I don't want to be ashamed to hold my book up in public. And I want it to look like the other covers I see in bookstores. So that means I will have to find a graphics person to both design the cover and prepare the artwork in final form to send to the printer with the copy.

Poynter's not much help here and I don't know any other publishers in the area, since none are listed in the "Yellow Pages." So I ask all nine typesetters if they can recommend or suggest the name of local or regional artfolk who design book covers. Four names emerge.

I call each and explain what I have in mind. One is too busy to consider it. The other three are interested; each has designed at least five covers. I tell them that it will take me at least a month to finalize the details, get bids from printers, and zero in on the cover copy, and at that point I'd like to make an appointment to see their work and discuss the project. But now I need one preliminary fact because I'm setting up the operating budget: the price or price range, and what determines the final expense.

They are understandably indirect, but the general range is from $500 to about $900. How long would it take? That is the biggest surprise. From a week to two months, depending. I'd need some firm deadlines here — and I'd better get to cover copy and design ideas early in the game.

Might as well leave the $1,000 in the budget and hope for a super, prize-winning cover at $500. In one week. And the winning lottery ticket too.

Illustrations. No guesswork here. I want my cousin, the drawer, to doodle about 20 cartoon-type illustrations to insert in the best places in the text. She's funny, draws very well, is a frustrated artist typing letters, and would pay me to get in a book. Best of all, she'll draw them to the size (or proportion so they can be reduced to size) that I need and will deliver them to me camera-ready. All I have to do is insert them in the text and off they go to the printer. I'll pay her $15 a final drawing. She says she'll do several for each concept and I can pick what I want for the final. She's bubbling with excitement. Me too. I saved $700, gave my cousin a break, and I'll get lively, fun artwork to lighten the book and give it some visual variety.

Printing and **Shipping**. Here I need some close figures, so I will send out a bid to a dozen specialty book printers. Poynter lists key ones in the appendix to *The Self-Publishing Manual,* and I can find out additional information from the *Literary Market Place* or John Kremer's *Directory of Short-Run Book Printers* (where they are evaluated). I use Poynter's bid form, "Request for Quotation: Book Printing & Binding," listing the total number of pages at 200, the trim size 6 x 9, and the quantity quotes at 1,500, 2,000, 3,000, and 5,000.

In three weeks I hear from nine of the 12. Since I'm following the "alley cat" approach in budgeting, I'm really interested in the 2,000 book bid now. The range of responses can be seen in the these three samples:

Publisher	A	B	C
Print price/2000	$ 2,782	3,225	5,331
Approx. freight	324	634	216
Total/print and ship	3,106	3,859	5,547
Cost per book	1.553	1.9295	2.7735
Shrinkwrap/book	.08	.07	.13

Since the other bids were between A and C in both total and per book cost, it is clear that in this case the "A" publisher is the least expensive. According to Kremer's book, it is also a solid, reputable firm. So I'm in good hands there.

My cost for printing: $2,782.

And for shipping: $324.

So that gives me these totals for the initial book production costs:

Research	$ 750
Overhead	0
Electronic teletypesetting	1,000
Cover preparation	1,000
Illustrations	300
Printing (2000 books)	2,782
Shipping	324
	$ 6,156

Fullfillment and tax/postage reserve fund

I'm inserting this out of order simply to remind you and me that these costs, an arbitrary $583 to pay the tax and postage for those who do not include it with their order and $1 a book for fulfillment (a total of $7,500 in this case), need not be paid in advance. The money can come from the order payments when they arrive, so we needn't worry about them now or, frankly, at all.

Promotional costs

On the other hand, these I must worry about very much. Without them I will sell as many books as I have friends, relatives, or handy buyers!

I have $14,000 maximum to invest, with $6,156 needed for initial costs. That leaves me $7,844 for promotion.

Flyer art preparation. I'm going to sell this book nationwide by a dynamite flyer that has recipients leaping for their checkbooks and excitedly awaiting delivery! Or something like that. Half of what creates that buying frenzy is the book itself, its title, and the dire need it meets. The other half — and the first in importance — is letting that needy audience know that my book exists, can help, and is immediately available.

So I need somebody to produce that flyer. What I know is principals — and what will make principals buy my book. What advertisers know is how to get recipients to respond, and how to design and prepare a flyer in camera-ready fashion for me to mail.

I call the Chamber of Commerce of the large city nearby and ask which companies sell by direct mail in their membership. I call their advertising managers, explain that I'm looking for the best person in town to prepare a direct mail brochure to sell a book. Whom would they suggest?

I do the same to both mailing houses in town, calling the order manager. Whose work is highly recommended by their clients? (I also ask them to send me any rate sheets they have since I will soon be at their doors with a major mailer.)

If I knew another publisher, I'd ask him or her for a recommendation. Finally, I check the advertising agencies and counselors in the "Yellow Pages." Nine are listed. A call to each tells me whether they specialize in display or direct mail advertising, and if they do the latter how often. Two fall out, another two sound distant and flaky. Of the remaining five three have been mentioned by the firms and the mailing houses. So I focus on them.

Each has an impressive list of clients and experience in related direct mail flyer preparation, so I get the names of the clients to cross-check. And a ball park figure. All come in well below $1,500. I keep it there nonetheless.

Which leaves me with $6,344 to print the fliers and get them distributed.

Print and mail fliers. Some quick calculations now to see just what I could mail for $6,344. Because I don't have the flyer ready and thus don't know its size, the paper quality, whether it will be one or multi-colored, and other essentials, I can't get a print bid yet. And the mailing house costs are in the air. If I wait too long, even postage fees will increase!

So I will fall back on the $ .37875 per flyer figure, which tells me that I could expect to have printed and delivered to my mailing list 16,750 fliers. Not bad. And if I sold at the 10% ratio, that would be 1,675 books at $15, or $25,125, minus $2,513 for fulfillment, or $22,612 in profit. I could invest all of that back in the mailing and send fliers to the rest of the 58,250 principals on my list — and have $550 left!

One problem: I had only 2,000 books printed and I've already sold 1,675. I'm going to need 5,500 more to meet the demand of the second mailing! Will they sell them to me for $550?

Since I paid for the first printing promptly, this time I'll check there print costs and request a 30-day payment, which is commonly given to established customers. In the original bid from publisher "A" the reprint cost for 5,000 books was $4,502, or $ .9004 each, so I might expect that for 5,500 I will have to pay about $ .88 each, or $4,840, plus another $800 for shipping. That would be $5,640. I must sell another 376 books to earn that much. If I don't sell that many books in the 30 days after I mail out 58,250 fliers I'm in deep, deep trouble with more than the printer!

I'm cutting it close putting every penny of that $14,000 I have into the project but if the figures I have projected hold true in a few months after the book is out, relying solely on direct mail, I expect to earn back $65,678 — or much more. That's the best scenario.

The worst scenario looks good too. Rather than needing a 10% buy ratio to get rich, I just need a 5.41% ratio to break even and get my $14,000 back. Two huge sighs of relief!

Fattening the alley cat

Putting all the selling weight on those fliers makes me very uncomfortable, particularly since my last $14,000 is sitting under that weight and in danger of disappearing forever!

How might I sell more books without any or much additional investment? Even better, what might I do that will push that magic 10% much higher?

In Chapter 8 we asked where the principals might buy this book. In addition to mail orders, I zeroed in on gatherings and oral presentations, and I found out if it were required or recommended for a class. All fine ideas but not much help right now, unless the regional meeting is soon to be held, I can get on the docket, and they'll let me distribute order forms after the talk. But it's still a slow, long shot. The mail is quicker.

Except for one other means we quickly discussed in Chapter 4: associations. We found seven groups for principals and four for superintendents and top school administrators, with a combined membership of 93,220. The best way for me to get on their pages is to have them review my book. If they'll include the cost and the ordering address in the review, the stars are right in heaven! Two things will happen: people who read the reviews will be much more likely to buy when they receive my flyer in the mail and some will place orders outright.

There's a way to be certain that my address is listed, the price noted, and the order solicited: run a display ad in the same issue, hopefully near the review.

Two steps take primary importance: (1) read the section in Poynter and get review copies, with proper accompaniment, in the right hands as quickly as possible, and (2) call the editors to check on whether they accept ads, and if so, get rates and follow through! The first is free; the latter I will pay from my initial $14,000, reducing the flyer preparation and mailing by the amount needed, which shouldn't be much. At first I would limit the display ads to small items in the NASSP, NAESP, AASA, and AFSA publications.

Another tack too: I'm going to check with editors of the publications we listed in that chapter (like the NAASP's *Bulletin* or *Tips for Principals*, the NAESP *Principal*, AASA's *The School Administrator*, or the AFSA *News*), through a query letter, to see if they would be interested in an article written directly to their readership about some facet of my book's theme to coincide with the book's release. In the article, or better in the biographical blurb near my name, I will insert pertinent ordering facts. I don't care if they pay for the article, which they probably don't do anyway. Just putting the concept before the readers as an excerpt or derivation of the just-released book will be worth its weight in gold, for immediate orders and later purchases.

And my friends. I'm going to sell this book like it's gilded. Because I believe it is. If I didn't think every principal would benefit plenty from reading my words I wouldn't publish it at all. My enthusiasm will infect the principals, who will tell friends, and that too will create a small but very much appreciated early groundswell. The idea is to get books sold, to earn money to get fliers printed, to mail to get books sold, and on and on. It is gilded.

11 PICKING A TITLE, CREATING TESTING TOOLS, AND TESTING YOUR BOOK – TWICE!

Nothing sells a book quicker than its title, particularly by mail. In one glance the title must explain what the book is about and why a person would want to buy it.

The title is the headline that gets its readers to want to read more. The hook that brings them in. It seizes their attention for the second that buys hours and hours of profitable reading. Or gets your book ignored.

So here is where you write down 10 to 25 or more possible titles as they come to mind. Only later, after the contents are fleshed out and you see what you're actually sharing with readers, must you select your final title.

Some title restraints

There are things to consider when selecting a title, though none is as important as this: "Without using deception, the title must sell the book."

Some titles do that better than others. They are usually short, catchy, accurate, and appropriate.

Short means just what it says: few words. Six or less are the easiest to remember. More than six usually requires the title to be run as a double-decker or, horrors, a triple-decker: lines atop each other on the flyer and cover. The problem is reader resistance if the title is long and dense. Yet many a good title has been long. Few are dense.

"Catchy" is just that. It catches your eye or ear. It twists a cliche or plays on a common phrase. A word or sound piques your interest. Yet many a good title isn't catchy. *Gone With the Wind* is; *The Holy Bible* or *The Torah* isn't.

Accurate gets to integrity. You don't want to sell a book through a title that misleads buyers into thinking the text is about something altogether different. And appropriate refers to tone. A formal academic text shouldn't be titled in vulgar slang. The language tone and theme of the book should be expressed in the words used in the title. *The Compleat (sic) Practical Joker* and *Gray's Anatomy* are appropriately titled.

You might consider using some of the 14 words said to be the most persuasive in the English language, if they would be accurate and appropriate: new, how to, save, discover, safety, health, free, you, guarantee, love, easy, money, proven, and results. These words demonstrate another point made by Winston Churchill, that when given choices seek old words rather than new, short words rather than long. Comfortable words known to the reader. Use polysyllabic jawbreakers at peril, unless that is what your book is about!

Finally, you cannot copyright a title, though in certain (rare) instances part or all of a title can be protected as a trademark. Others' titles are usable by you, as your title can be purloined by them. Best to plow new ground, though, to avoid any confusion another's title might create.

Why do you need a title now, even if you might, on the long shot, change it later to bring it closer to the book's contents? Because you want to test the book before you invest any more time or money and you can't test a book without some title!

Two kinds of test marketing

You want to write and produce a book that will sell to a maximum number of people for minimum promotional cost. You also want to do that in the best, quickest, and most profitable way. Therefore you need two tests:

(1) To see what percentage of your target market will buy your book at what cost.
(2) To see what form of publishing is best for you.

Which form of publishing best meets your needs?

We must reconsider both forms of publishing again at this step.

To reiterate, in standard commercial publishing a firm accepts a manuscript, produces and prints it as a book, sells it, and pays the writer a percentage of what it earns for each book sold.

By the other process the writer writes a book, produces it, usually has the printing done elsewhere, receives the bound volumes, and sells them. Called self-publishing, the writer's profits come after expenses have been paid.

Sometimes there is a mix of the two. A standard publisher may buy a writer's books in final, printed form and distribute them. A writer may decide to reprint a book that was earlier produced and sold by a publisher and went out of print. Or the writer may contract with a standard publisher to buy back a certain number of books to sell to his or her own market. At this step let's focus on the unmixed examples of commercial versus self-publishing, plus the last type of mix.

Sometimes there is no choice at all. The standard publishers aren't interested in the writer's book. Or they might be interested if the contents were slanted differently or written to a different readership, but the writer is adamant that the book will be done one way for one particular readership — so self-publishing has only one alternative: no publishing at all.

Therefore, to determine which form of publishing is best, you must first see if any standard publisher is interested, then calculate the likely income from each. Or you may simply decide that self-publishing is it. Now is when the choice, if any, is made.

How to test standard publishers

First, why would you test them?

Because if you can get standard publishers to do the editing, printing, promotion, and marketing and still receive what you wish for your writing labors, you will save enough time to write another book — or do anything else equally as exciting — while they tend to the publishing chores!

Secondarily, if they are willing to invest their money and pay you big returns, they predict sufficiently large sales to pay themselves a far greater return. Which may tell you that self-publishing would be even more profitable for you! (I have a friend who will not self-publish a book that a standard publisher doesn't want; he relies on their gut reaction and testing, as it is, to tell him if he has a winner!)

What do publishers want to know? The current *Writer's Market* is the best guide. It lists about 100 pages of publishers, each telling in detail what they publish and how (or if) they want to be approached.

For the most part you will use one of two approaches, (1) a book proposal for many bids, and (2) a query letter with attachments for one-at-a-time solicitations.

While bidding by proposal, by sending simultaneous queries and a sample chapter to many publishers, covers far more ground much quicker, it is so seldom successful for newcomers that I will simply suggest a book for you to follow should you wish to pursue that route: Michael Larsen's *How To Write a Book Proposal*, published by Writer's Digest Books.

The most successful route is, alas, the slowest. But it shows you to best advantage and allows you to market your idea before and while you write the actual book.

It requires you to select a topic, then answer five basic questions:

(1) Who would read your book?
(2) Why would they buy it?
(3) Where would they use it?
(4) What else is available?
(5) How does your book differ?

Particularly important is that you know the standard publishers working your target market, as well as those books similar to yours in the current *Subject Guide to Books in Print* and *Forthcoming Books*. Those will be the markets you want to approach first.

Review your working question. Your book will be the answer to it. Around that theme and the replies to the five basic questions above, write a two-page query letter to the publisher you would most like to handle your book. Query publishers one at a time, in decreasing preference.

Since you have already studied your market closely and have an idea of how to sell to it, include that information in your query — or on an attached page. Be specific with numbers and facts: the size of your target market, of other markets with similar interests, the need your book meets, what other books exist that address that need, how yours does it better (and why). But don't include your promotional tool or ideas you have about non-book means by which you can also sell that information.

With the query send (1) an outline of your book's contents or an annotated table of contents, (2) a one-page synopsis, if necessary, and (3) a reference/resource sheet that explains the major printed sources you will draw from for your book's contents, in annotated bibliographical fashion, and the people you will interview, in annotated biographical form.

Do you mention that you want to receive $50,000 profit from the royalties (and double that on your own later by non-book means)? Not the doubling, and perhaps not the $50,000 either. First you want them to reply affirmatively, then you can talk money.

Using our $15 book and the 10%-12.5%-15% of list royalties as a base, the standard publisher would have to sell 24,723 copies for you to realize your $50,000. Will your target market yield that kind of a sale? Will the publisher sell directly to that market, preferably by mail? And if the publisher does sell by mail, will you receive a lower royalty?

If your query and attachments get you to the money-talking stage, you need to know those things, plus:

(1) When do you receive royalties? Quarterly? Annually
(2) How much is withheld each time for returns and damages?
(3) When will the book appear? What happens if, between approval of the final, corrected manuscript and its publication the publisher aborts the book?
(4) What unchangeable stipulations exist in the contract about rights to future books or the use of the information of the book in question?
(5) How much of the budget will be pegged for promotion to the target market? When and how will it be used?
(6) What track record does this firm have with other writers of similar books? (The last point can be easily checked: contact them directly and ask.)

In the meantime, the publisher, in receipt of your package, will judge your idea, marketing figures, and writing skills from what is at hand. If impressed, you will likely be asked to send several (usually three) sample chapters. If still interested, a contract is generally drawn. Your advance (against royalties) is paid in part when the contract is signed, in part when the final corrected manuscript is submitted, and (at times) when the book is actually published.

Package your idea to highlight its value, need, and marketability and usually you will find one (or many) publishers eager to run the risk, do the selling, and keep 85-90% of the gross income.

Those are the realities. One excellent source that talks about commercial publishing from the inside, and applies directly to the discussion here, is Bell's *How To Get Your Book Published*, by Writer's Digest Books. For a more complete, step-by-step explanation (with examples) of the selling approach to standard publishers, attend my seminar (or buy the tape series and workbook of the same) called "Before You Write That Book...."

Let me insert here one of several ways that double-win thinking and clear contracting might help offset the huge financial sacrifice one makes to have others publish their book(s).

A double win: buying back books from a standard publisher

Sometimes a "deal" can be made with a standard publisher so you can sell your book at a higher profit to a selected market.

Let's say that you offer seminars and those who attend are unlikely to be influenced by the publisher's promotional campaign. You may want to buy a set number of books to sell directly to that group.

The conventional, and far less profitable, way is simply to buy them as needed from the publisher. The standard discount starts at 40% for ten or more, and can go up to 50% for large quantities. Often a publisher will not pay you your royalty on those purchases, so one concession you might seek in your contract is to receive both the conventional wholesaler's discount and your royalty.

A better "deal" follows the system often used by book clubs. As a book is being printed book clubs buy an additional number of books from that same printing, thus lowering the publisher's per-book printing cost while reducing their own cost. They then pay the publisher 10% of the cost of the book to their own club members, and agree to limit sales exclusively to that group.

For example, say that the book would cost $1 each if 5,000 were printed. The book club orders 3,000 more, lowering everybody's cost to $ .91 per book. If the book sold at $9.95 list, the book club might sell it at $7.95 to its members. They would then pay the publisher 10% of $7.95, or $ .795, plus $.91 per book, plus shipping to their warehouse (let's say $ .165 a book) — or a total of $1.87 a book. The book costs them less than 20% of list; that is, they receive better than an 80% discount.

If you know that you can sell a hefty number of books within a year or two to your seminar participants you may strike a similar agreement with your publisher. Pay for your copies of the book from your advance against royalties. Of course you won't receive royalties for the books you sell and the publisher will probably ask you to agree in writing to limit the sales specifically to the markets you suggest (and thus not compete openly with the publisher), but those are acceptable conditions for such a profit ratio.

How would that work with our example and still earn you $50,000?

Let's say that you want to order 2,000 copies of the book to sell at $15, the list price. To simplify the calculations, let's say that:

(1) the production cost of the book is $1.50

(2) the publisher insists that you pay 10% of the list price, or another $1.50

(3) shipping costs are $500

So your cost for 2,000 books is $6,500. And your potential income is $30,000 (2,000 x $15). Your profit would be $23,500.

Tightly-Targeted Markets

To make up the difference of your $50,000, you need to earn $26,500 in royalties. Thus, at $15 and the 10%-12.5%-15% on list payments, the publisher must sell 14,278 books.

By assuming some of the marketing yourself you not only increase your profit ratio and lower the book's production costs for the standard publisher, you lower by more than 8,000 the number of books that must be sold for you to realize your goal of $50,000 from the book. Everybody wins — as long as you sell your 2,000 copies and the publisher sells the 14,278!

Testing your book in your target market

The best way to see if anybody in your target market will buy your book is to ask them. Simple.

But not so simple.

If you know people in the target market, can you trust their responses — or will they say yes because you are friends? If you don't know them, how do you know that they are representative of the larger market? Is there a danger that somebody you tell will beat you to the market with their issue of your book? And how can you find out how much people will really pay: given choices, won't everybody pick the lowest price?

To select people to be tested, keep the number fairly small and limit yourself to the target market. You already know how they can be found by mailing list, but generally the minimum number of names the list renter will provide is several thousand or the minimum cost is $100+. Nonetheless, you might contact the mailing list manager and explain what you are doing: you will rent their full list later but you'd like to test a sample (say 50-200) now, and could you secure those names on pressure-sensitive labels for a low, introductory price? Sometimes they will agree!

Usually they won't, so then you must pick (a) friends, (b) others in the target market suggested by friends, or (3) target market members chosen in other ways.

Friends, as suggested earlier, aren't too reliable. They would rather tell you what you want to hear than what they really feel. And who has 50-200 friends from a target market? Still, there are friends who will understand why objectivity is so important and they should be asked.

Friends' friends are often a better source, particularly if the person recommending them doesn't talk about the survey first.

Perhaps the best way is to use a list of members in the target market (such as an association membership list, names from club rosters, professional listings in the phone book, etc.). If your book is to be national in scope, this also allows you to test in various areas of the United States. There is no way to be certain that what this test group says represents all of the other members of the target market, of course. But the larger your test group, the more likely it will be fairly representative.

How do you protect the idea of your book? In truth, there is no way to protect an idea other than to keep it to yourself. So you must take a risk if you want to see if others will buy your book, since to respond they must know what the book is about.

Avoid including certain people in the group tested: association officers or others with widespread market contacts, all media folk, seminar-givers or book writers in the field, or anybody else you suspect might put your idea or information in print.

And keep the number tested small and select, make your presentation to them professional in tone and appearance, imply that the book is nearly ready for release, and tell them only what is necessary for them to make a valid response.

What will you send them? First determine what you want to know. Probably whether they would be interested at some future date in buying a book about your subject at a stated price.

Draw from your promotional tool, your title, and whatever else you know or imagine about your book and prepare an information sheet that describes your book's purpose, contents, length (pick an approximate length that is divisible by four), cost, type of binding (cloth or paperback), and illustrations. It needn't be designed to sell the book nor must it contain an example of the final cover or your photo. Simply enough information, particularly about the contents and benefits, to give the recipient a solid grasp of what you will produce.

Then compose a letter to accompany the information sheet in which you ask its recipient for a favor, a quick one-minute reply to the questions on the enclosed questionnaire. That can be a postcard or a 3" x 5" index card with a self-addressed envelope. Explain in the letter that you are in the final stages of completing work on the book described on the enclosed information sheet and simply need a sense of the target market's response so the book can be designed to meet the needs of those most interested in purchasing it.

What you want to know you ask on the questionnaire. The format most likely to be responded to will ask 2-5 questions, short and straightforward, followed by reply boxes to be marked. You might also leave room for additional comments. Ask them please to return this card by mail today! Thank them in the letter and on the questionnaire. And don't include a place for their name or address; if they wish, they can write that in.

Finally, if you use an index card, include a #9 return envelope with your name and address on the front. Put an actual stamp on both the return and the original mailing envelope — some say that several stamps will increase the response even more.

How do you test the price? Gently. One way is to give the respondent a choice of three different prices on the reply card. Another is to divide your test market into three equal groups, trying to give each group the same geographic spread. Then you send the same information sheet to each group except that one group has the book priced at x, the second at Y, and the third at Z. The latter approach will generally give a more accurate response if the test group is sufficiently large.

All that remains is to see if the positive replies exceed, equal, or fall short of the percentage of potential buying return you need to realize the kind of profit you want. If it exceeds or equals that percentage, charge ahead. If it falls short, you must find out why. Is it the test? The price? The subject? The book's contents? The timing?

If it falls far short, now is the best time to alter or abort the book, before hard work and hard cash come into play.

Do you run both tests at the same time?

Why not? Test standard publishers to see if they will publish the book, when, what they will pay, and how well you and they can market your words.

And test the tightly-targeted market to see if 10% of them will buy your book, at what cost level, and what profits you might expect that way.

Then make a choice.

Two things are certain: you won't know about the standard publishers unless you ask, and you don't want to risk the high promotional costs of self-publishing until you have a solid sense of the likely buying ratio and rate.

Get to it!

EXAMPLE

Picking my title

Now I need a title that does it all: tells what the book is about and why it should be bought immediately. Preferably a short, catchy, accurate, and appropriate title. One that will get attention and action. It must sell my book.

But first I'm going to write down every title that comes to mind, then worry about the qualifications or restraints later. Here goes:

(a) Principals, You Flunk!
(b) They Don't Shoot Old Principals, Do They?
(c) Life During and After Principalship
(d) TILT: Getting and Keeping a Principal's Life in Balance
(e) Principals: What Happened to the Real You?
(f) Principals: Refinding Your Own Life
(g) Principals: How To Find Your Family, Fun, Fire, Fortune, and a Fascinating Future While the Teachers Teach, the Kids Bloom, and the Buildings Bulge!
(h) Principals: How To Create The Whole You
(i) Principals: Making You a Whole Person Every Hour of Every Day
(j) Principals: How To Bloom Even When the Halls Are Empty, the Kids are Gone, and Yours is the Last Car in the Lot
(k) Principals: Getting It Together— A Private Life Worth Living!
(l) Principals: Where's the Real You In and Out of School?
(m) Principals: Earn an A+ by Defining and Creating a Brighter, Richer, and Happier You!
(n) A Whole Principal: A Better School
(o) Even Principals Only Live Once: Making Your Private Side Bloom!

These 15 titles took days to compose and are the survivors of perhaps 80 tries. (My best ideas generally come a day or two after I get to the task, usually when I'm running or my mind is in idle, so I need a writing pad nearby most of the time. I start writing things down right away, though, to speed up the interval between those "days afterward.") Let's look at the offerings in greater detail.

Hardly a short one in the lot. They're to the point and accurate — or will be when I bring the book's contents into line. Some are catchy, but "appropriate" bothers me the most. They could be academic and stuffy. Yet I'm trying to appeal to the other side of the same person, the out-of-school or school-plus angle, and I think that the less pedantic and highly structured the title sounds, the more it expresses what I want. It may get more attention too.

I also put the word "Principal" as close to the front of each title as I could. Poynter suggests that the first word of the title be the subject of the book so it is easy to find in the index. In TCE marketing that is doubly important. Here the title tells the targeted market that the book is written solely to and about them, addressing their needs directly, with examples they can relate to.

The hardest is picking just one title to test. My inclinations are to choose (g) or (m). So much for shortness!

"Principals: Earn an A+ by Defining and Creating a Brighter, Richer, and Happier You!" blends a rather academic structure with four benefits every principal wants: brightness, wealth, happiness, and an A+. It is a bit clever. And just a hair flat.

So my final choice is (g), "Principals: How To Find Your Family, Fun, Fire, Fortune, and a Fascinating Future While the Teachers Teach, the Kids Bloom, and the Buildings Bulge!" It includes all of the benefits I will write about — the five F's — in a fun way while being just outlandish enough, in length and reverence, to get their attention. Principals are readers so the many words worry me less than whether they can find something there that they want to change. One element reads oddly— "Find Your Family." As if the family were lost, but in context I think it makes sense and I can't think of another way to phrase it that works as well. I envision this graphically with the key words in bold, stacked — PRINCIPALS:, FAMILY, FUN, FIRE, FORTUNE, and FASCINATING FUTURE — and the rest in smaller type in between, highlighting the hooks with which I want to ensnare them.

Should I test market both ways?

Why not? Though I intend to self-publish this book, if a standard publisher would grab onto the theme with fervor and give me a fast, fat contract I'd be very happy, thank you, to pump out the text and let them put out the books and do the promotion while I launched into a second book! Even if a standard publisher is mildly interested, it will show me that he thinks there is money to be made here, which would encourage me to promote my own book with greater vigor.

Testing standard publishers

I'm going to send my query with attachments to one publisher at a time. But which first? I check the current *Subject Guide to Books in Print* and *Forthcoming Books* and there is absolutely nothing about this topic now or soon to be in print. So I look at school-directed books in general and see who is serving that market, then I list the publishers by the number of books published in the past three years. If they are actively working a market, they are my best hope. Finally, I check the writeup of the first (the most active) on the list in the current *Writer's Market*, tailor my letter to those needs, prepare attachments, and off the bundle goes.

Three elements will be sent in that "package": (1) a query letter two pages long, (2) an outline of the proposed book, and (3) a reference/resource sheet. Since the focus of this book is self-publishing, I won't develop examples of (1) and (3) here, referring you to my book *Query Letters/Cover Letters: How They Sell Your Writing* (see the last page in this book) for similar examples. The outline appears later in this chapter.

If the editor is interested, I will probably have to send sample chapters, generally three. Sometimes the editor suggests a different approach or outline; often he/she wants one segment emphasized rather than another. All before contract numbers are mentioned, though I have a general understanding of what they pay and when from the *Writer's Market*. Since I'm writing the book by that time anyway, it is easy to send what is requested.

Am I afraid the editor will turn me down and assign the same topic to another writer? Or steal from my actual writing for somebody else's book? Not at all. In the first case, I will be published long before a copycat publisher. In the second, I only pray that their book is very, very successful so my lawsuit will be very, very profitable.

When do I decide whether to accept a standard publishing contract or to self-publish? If it's even a possibility, the latest point at which I can select is before I have the manuscript finally proofed, typeset, and pasted and before I invest much money in promotion. But after I have done my own test marketing, so I have comparative facts upon which to make a sound decision.

A last question: what about buying books back from the publisher in this case? It's a great idea but only when I have a reliable outlet or buyers for those books' sale, such as at a seminar or speech. In this case, as we have already seen in Chapter 7, there are few opportunities to offer seminars to gathered principals, and while offering speeches would be more likely, the sponsoring structure doesn't encourage commercial hawking afterwards in either case. It wouldn't make financial sense here unless I wanted to sell in large scale by mail. If I'm going to do that, why not publish the book myself and keep far more of the profit?

Testing my book in the targeted market

What I must do now is create a testing tool to send to 200 principals across the U.S.

But first I must find the 200, so I turn to my mailing list managers to see if I can rent, borrow, or simply get that many test names without having to dig them out and type them myself. Bingo! One of the managers will run a sample 200 names, Nth selection (noted), for his cost of $12 (including shipping to me) on pressure-sensitive labels. On the understanding I will rent a fuller list from him later. A deal.

Now I must put together something fetching yet accurate that will give me a true sense of whether I can sell my book to 10% or more of the mailing list.

The information sheet

I've already prepared a rather simple contents outline for the query package sent to the standard publisher, so that can also be included in the information sheet sent to my test market. Like the title, I composed the basic outline, then spent days fidgeting with it to include all I must in the best order. This is the result:

    I. The life of a principal.
        A. The problems of getting there
        B. The frustrations of staying there.
        C. The difficulties of growing through and beyond.
    II. What happened to the real you?
    III. Serving with love and real dedication while learning to say no.
    IV. Injecting the five "F's" to create a brighter, richer and happier you:
        A. Family.
        B. Fun.
        C. Fire.
        D. Fortune.
        E. Future.
    V. Getting (back) in balance.
    VI. Everybody wins as you grow!

INFORMATION SHEET

PRINCIPALS:

How To Find Your Family, Fun, Fire, Fortune, and a Fascinating Future While the Teachers Teach, the Kids Bloom, and the Buildings Bulge!

by Gordon Lee Burgett

Being a principal's not enough!

There's about 75,000 of us keepin' our noses clean, doing our best, and trying to juggle our own lives, kids, and dreams — certain that most of the time we're losing on every front!

Me too! Between the students, faculty, staff, parents, townfolk, bank, obituary column, my waistline, and galloping wrinkles it dawned on me that I'd better get my act together and strike some happy compromise between me the principal and me the person, parent, and dreamer or I'd wake up some morning retired and too damn worn out to care!

That's what this book is all about.

I wondered if any principal anywhere was as capable and contented outside their school as they were in. So I hunted for them: principals leading super, full, complete, exciting, challenging lives — and great schools.

And there they were, hiding in every corner of America, looking remarkably like us! All sizes and shapes, both sexes, and most were true magicians: on a principal's wage they managed to save for a comfortable retirement without sacrificing during their prime years! I interviewed them and in this book I share their secrets, plus a wealth of related research, to help us take a hard look at where we are, where we could be, and sensible, step-by-step ways we can take to get there.

Principals are people too. We deserve to be 100% of our dreams. And we all deserve a copy of this book!

CONTENTS

I. The life of a principal.
  A. The problems of getting there.
  B. The frustrations of staying there.
  C. The difficulties of growing through and beyond.
II. What happened to the real you?
III. Serving with love and real dedication while learning to say no.
IV. Injecting the five "F's" to create a brighter, richer, and happier you:
  A. Family.
  B. Fun.
  C. Fire.
  D. Fortune.
  E. Future.
V. Getting (back) in balance.
VI. Everybody wins as you grow!

PUBLICATION DATE: May, 199X

GORDON BURGETT

has been a principal for 18 years, winner of the State of California "Distinguished Educators" award in 1987, a six-session legislative liaison assistant to the state Senate, a former football and track coach, author of six books in the educational field, and a keynote speaker nationwide for the past decade. He has two daughters, his original wife, a Nissan pickup truck, a sore knee, and about 10 years before the knackers come knocking. Did he write this book in time?

Bassman-Willer Press
P.O. Box 6405
Santa Maria, CA 93456

POSITIVE MONEY-BACK GUARANTEE

I understand that if I am not completely satisfied with this book I may return the undamaged copy within 10 days for a complete refund of the purchase price.

$14.95, plus $1 shipping
(200 pages/paperback)

ISBN 0-9605078-9-8
LC #9X-61718

Tightly-Targeted Markets

The rest of my information sheet will consist of the title and byline, the date of publication box, length/cost/binding info, several paragraphs of explanatory prose, and some biographical data about the author — the things I would want to know before shelling out $14.95.

Some of the information is guesswork. I figure it will take me a maximum six months to have the book out, so about nine months hence becomes the publication date. I guess at the length of 200 pages; nobody will complain if it runs longer, and I'll make sure it isn't shorter! I expect to print in paperback. As for the cost, my calculations show that about $15 is the least I can sell it for and make the profit I want. (Incidentally, that is in line with the six to ten times the unit production cost ratio commonly charged for trade books.) But just to see if the market might be willing to pay more, I will test 100 at $14.95 (plus $1/shipping), plus another 50 at $17.50, shipping included, and a final 50 at $19.95, shipping included.

The need to insert biographical information presents me with an enigma. I chose the example I am developing because it is easily understandable by any reader and, with the proper adaptation to your field, would be as easily applied to your needs. I don't intend to actually write this book but have researched it and interviewed principals so that what I say is as accurate as I can make it. In truth, my most relevant educational background was as an associate professor, administrator, and dean at the university level, plus two years of occasional substitute teaching at grades 4-12. So I am forced either to use my own background, which to principals reading the information sheet wouldn't be much of a selling draw, or to create here, for the purposes of developing an information sheet much as it would or should look, a bio insert that would be appropriate for a person who would indeed write this book. I've chosen the latter, for instructional purposes only. Your biographical insert must be correct and, if questioned, verifiable.

What remains, then, is prose tying the title to the other material.

On page 125 you saw the result of my having brought these elements together to create an Information Sheet.

The questionnaire letter

Since the information sheet must be accompanied by some explanatory letter, I address that next. More people will read a short letter than a long one. It must be clear, concise, and tell what I want, why, and what's in it for them. Finally, it must look sharp and professional — but not too slick. (Note that I have created a name for my publishing house. You must do the same so this letter comes from the publisher but is written by you.) Here's my creation:

Bassman-Willer Press
P.O. Box 6405
Santa Maria, CA 93456
March x, 19xx

Dear Principal:

I've been a principal for 18 years, dancing to the superintendent's often atonal tune, holding my breath as I ring the fire alarm, watching teachers bud while the older students bloom, rejoicing when our graduates enter UCLA or join the Navy or police force or do anything that makes our modest, collective efforts worth the while....

And now I've written a book about the other side of our lives, and how we can make that richer (and ourselves in the process)! The book is called <u>Principals: How To Find Your Family, Fun, Fire, Fortune, and a Fascinating Future While the Teachers Teach, the Kids Bloom, and the Buildings Bulge!</u> The enclosed information sheet tells more about the book's contents.

Would you help me? It will take less than a minute. We're conducting a random market test of 200 principals throughout the United States. All we want to know is the answer to the first three items on the enclosed questionnaire. (The fourth gives you an opportunity to make suggestions or share thoughts, if you wish.) Simply place three "x's" now and put the card in the enclosed, stamped envelope and mail it. That's it!

I can't reward you and retain the anonymity of the response, and I'm sorry about that. But I am grateful, and I sincerely thank you for your kindness and help.

Respectfully,

Gordon Burgett

Incidentally, I will be able to trace the three price tests because each returned questionnaire will have the respective price on it. (I'll print 100 at the lowest price and 50 each of those in higher categories.) But if I want to test the responses by geographic category I can do that by the stamps on the #9 return envelope sent in each mailing. If I divide the U.S. into five sections, I might use 25-cent stamps for one section, a 10- and 15-cent combination for the second, a 15- and 10-cent combination for the third (simply reversing the order), and the last two by switching 5- and 20-cent stamps.

The test questionnaire

I really want to know one thing: will they buy the damn book at what I want to charge? So that is question #1. Then I'd like to know if any or many would buy at it for $3 more in hardback (or cloth). If so, later I'll give all buyers that choice. Finally, how would they most likely buy it. A fourth point gives them the opportunity to share suggestions on the back.

Thus the questionnaire, on a printed 3" x 5" card, would look like this:

---

(1) I ( ) would   buy **Principals: How To Find Your Family, Fun, Fire,**
( ) would not   **Fortune, and a Fascinating Future While the**
Teachers Teach, the Kids Bloom, and the Buildings
Bulge! for $14.95, plus $1 shipping.

(2) I ( ) would   prefer to buy this book in a hard cover edition
( ) would not   costing $3 more.

(3) I would most likely buy this book ( ) by mail, ( ) at a conference or convention, ( ) from a card deck mailed to my office, ( ) by word-of-mouth, or ( ) _____.

(4) On the other side of this card I have written suggestions or thoughts I want to share.

Many thanks.

Mail and hold my breath!

All that's left is to send the mailing out and see what returns. I will know a series of things by whatever comes back:

(1) Does this show a 10% or more buying response at $14.95, plus $1? At $17.50? At $19.95?
(2) At which level will I earn the greatest return from book sales? Where will I likely sell the most books?

(3) Should I offer the book in both paper and cloth?
(4) Which of the buying means most appealed to the principals? Are they unresponsive to other means?
(5) Would another test — same size/larger — be prudent before continuing?

Now I must evaluate the data and make a major, real-money decision. Will I publish this book myself or either have it published by another house or abandon it?

The results — and a decision!

Let's say that the results from my test were as follows: an 11% positive response at $14.95, 5% at $17.50, and 4.5% at $19.50. Nine said they would prefer to buy the hard cover version at $3 more, all of whom received the $14.95 book info sheet. Almost all would buy by mail and at conventions. Only four responded to card decks: do they know that terminology? And some had suggestions. The two most common: good luck and shorten the title!

Thus at $14.95 with an 11% response I would sell 8,250 books to a targeted market of 75,000 principals. Figuring half of that $14.95 as profit, I should earn $61,668.75. For $17.50 and $19.50, the profit should be, respectively, $32,812.50 and $32,906.25.

If I sent the questionnaire featuring the $14.95 book to 100 recipients and nine said they would consider buying the cloth version at $3 more, let me assume that only half would in fact buy that book at $17.95 (which is similar to the 5% who would buy it at $17.50). If my profit is still 50% of $17.95 and I could expect to sell to 4.5% of my targeted market (or 3,375 of 75,000), that would earn $30,290.63. Then subtracting that 4.5% from the 11% total who indicated that they would buy the $14.95 book, my profit by offering this book in paper (at $14.95) and cloth (at $17.95) would be $66,730.63. — $5,061.88 more.

Two other indications: I'm on line selling this by mail and at gatherings. And while only 2% of the 200 tested responded to card decks as a means through which they would buy this book, that translates to 1,500 sales or $12,133.50 using the same paper/cloth ratios above.

Do I believe the returns enough to spend a bundle for this book's promotion? They are likely higher than I will actually sell since these principals have been specifically asked to respond, lessening their inertia and inaction.

Yet I think they are in the shooting range. And a 10% sales rate is very likely. So, yes, I will think in terms of selling about 4,500 books in paper, 2,000 in cloth (though will initially have only 1,000 bound this way), and hope for 800 more sales by card deck. Even trimming my expectations back to these levels my profits should be $58,058.70.

While no standard publisher has shown interest in the book, none will bring me these returns anyway. And since I need to sell to only about 5% of the principals just to break even, there's a lot of cushion between 5% and 11%.

I'll continue. From here on I play with the striped chips. Big gamble time — two aces and a king in my hand with two cards to draw!

12 GATHERING INFORMATION AND WRITING THE BOOK

You've tested your idea and title one or two ways, the results are in, and you want to self-publish your book—great! Now comes the real work.

At this step you must write a book that is worth far more than $14.95 to the buyer. To do that you must plan precisely what the book will say, figure out how and when you will gather its facts and quotes, set up a writing schedule you will adhere to, put the words on paper, have them proofed, and edit that prose into final form.

A recustomizing before you hunt for the words

In Chapter 6 you began the customizing process. Since then you have determined what promises the book must keep, given the work a title, devised a tentative table of contents, and brought the project into a distinct form.

Now the earlier steps must be further refined.

Your purpose statement, necessarily general at that time, must now be sharpened to match this book's specific topic. That will change the working question. The secondary questions will likewise become sharper.

Then a review of the books that you surveyed must be done again. You will want to study in depth those books that bear directly on your final topic. And you may have to search deeper and wider for additional information.

As you progress, fill in and adjust the outline from the table of contents. Determine how each chapter will be written, including:

(1) the order in which its facts, quotes, anecdotes, and other items will be used.

(2) the sources of those items: references, resources, own experiences or observations, etc.

(3) the kinds and sources of all illustrations

Determine the perspective, the angle, that you as the author will take in relation to the material and the reader. Are you an expert sharing expertise?

An information gatherer and explainer? Is the material to be presented objectively or subjectively?

If your position is that of an expert, what must you do to reinforce or enhance the buyer's perception of your expertise? Join an association? Get licensed? Renew or update your license? Publish or speak to gain more, wider, or better exposure?

There are other ways to enhance you, your expertise, or your book. Would a foreword by an expert in the field help? Or co-authoring with another person with wider recognition? Sometimes a companion workbook lends value to the major text. And testimonials on the front or back cover, or both, can greatly add to a book's professional acceptability, as can testimonials on the flyer.

The role of illustrations and how they will be coordinated with the copy must be considered now. If illustrations are needed for your pages, are any of those that are used in other sources suitable and accessible? What will they cost? Will the rights' holder permit their use? Or can the illustrations be developed or purchased elsewhere or in another way? Where? When? Cost?

Finally, at every step you must continually ask, "Does this book satisfy the expectations of and promises made to the buyer?"

Some very basic thoughts about getting information and starting to write your book

Very basic. Start by checking the key word of your topic in an encyclopedia. While you know some things about the topic there are gaps to be filled. And since there are gaps, you don't know what you don't know. Thus, start from an assumption of zero knowledge, skim what you understand, search for rudimentary elements you never fully grasped plus anything else that is new, and work from the center outward.

The card catalog in the library is a great place to begin your hunt for written information. You've done much of this in Chapter 6. Go back again for a second hunt. Follow the numbering to the stacks to find other books that address your topic. Copy and investigate the bibliographies of the books that deal directly with your subject. Check again the *Subject Guide to Books in Print* and *Forthcoming Books*. Try different libraries: university, city, specialized. You can secure virtually any book in print through the interlibrary loan system. Ask at the desk.

Often a ton of good information hides in newspapers and magazines. Check periodicals indexes; ask for the microfilm, microfiche, or old copies, and dig in. Newspaper indexes are helpful. Remember that virtually every academic discipline has its own index, each with hundreds of obscure journals listed.

Check Alden Todd's *Finding Facts Fast*, or similar how-to-use-the-library guides, if you are uncertain. And ask the angels of the stacks, the reference librarians.

As for interviews, there are books about the technique but little mystery. Know something about each person you wish to interview before you make the contact, know basically what you want from that interview, prepare your questions in a logical order, then ask. Interview in person or by phone. Seek permission before you tape, if you do. Tell the people why you are interviewing them. Get to the point quickly — and let them talk. Finally, be accurate in quoting. If you don't understand something, ask for another explanation. If you miss a response, ask the informant to repeat it.

When you have enough library material (references) and live material (resources), convert that into copy. Arrange it in some order, match it to your outline, and begin typing. Don't worry about spelling or grammar, just get the material down. Work a section, then a chapter at a time. Set a schedule and keep to it. Then ask what is missing for full comprehension or presentation — get it and write it in.

Look at the order. Does it make sense? Does it flow well? Can the reader understand it? Move sections around, switch sentences, play with the text until it strikes the best balance. Then check spelling and grammar. Bingo, you have the first draft!

One way to record information

To write a book you need reliable information close at hand. Often that comes from many scattered places — and your computer is stationary and far from libraries, field, interview source, or other fonts of that needed material.

So you go to the information, take notes, bring them back, sort them, and keep writing. Let me suggest one way to record those notes that will bring you maximum return for the time invested.

First, though, what do you record them on? Some use legal pads, keeping the items on separate sheets by topic or source. Some just write things down in the order in which they occur or are found, also on legal pads. Others prefer to isolate each idea or point on 3 x 5" index cards. That is up to you. But whatever you use, you must clearly identify the origin of everything noted; that is, you must tie each point to its source. (If you are the source, write "me.")

It becomes tedious having to list the full source of each point made. So here's a way to simplify that. Say that you have five legal pads. On the top of each pad you write one of the following: (1) **facts**, (2) **references**, (3) **resources**, (4) **expert bio info**, or (5) **related topics**.

Then every time you get a fact that you think pertinent to your book, you write that fact on the (1) fact legal pad (or index card). If that came from a written source, the first time you use that source you pull out your (2) reference pad and you write down the full bibliographical information: author, title, publisher, place of publication, and date. You also give that written source its own letter, say "A." Then on the fact sheet, after the fact from that source, you also write "A" followed by the page number, say "A-17." (If there are several volumes, like an encyclopedia, you might list the volume too.) Thereafter, every time you use that same source you need only put its identifying letter and the page (and volume) number. At any future time you can instantly return to the origin of that written information to verify, recheck, whatever.

But let's say your source isn't written, it's oral: an interview, radio talk, tape, or speech. Again, the facts go on the fact sheet (or index card). But the source is noted on the (3) resources sheet, used here to mean oral resources. You simply note all that is needed to pin that fact back to its origin. Perhaps "Michael Jackson radio talk show, 1/23/89, 10-11, KABC, interview with Ivan Rasputin." And you give that a Roman numeral, say "II." (You must avoid the letters that are also commonly used Roman numerals: I, V, and X.) On the fact sheet you simply note II. Or if there are a series of interviews, on the fact sheet you note the Roman numeral and the date.

The (4) expert bio info pad is where you will build up a list and biography of those quoted or cited who are experts in the field of your research. Divide this pad alphabetically. Perhaps Dr. David Jones is an expert often quoted. Under "J" you will list his name, followed by every biographical fact you can gather each time he is cited or quoted (noting the source with the letter or Roman numeral). You can supplement this later, if necessary, from a current "*Who's Who*" or similar library biographical listing. Why bother? Because at some point you may wish to interview this expert, for the book or spinoff articles, and this gives you a list of potential interviewees as well as information at hand about them.

And (5) related topics is where you note every spinoff idea, every new angle, every unique approach, anything that will let you expand your production and earnings from information gathered. Also, this is where you note other ways the information can be used: by other means, by combining means, and soon. One way to encourage the latter is to title pages on this pad by the other means: articles, seminars, speeches, audio tapes, consulting, etc. so that when you think of another way to use the information there is a place where it and like ideas can be noted.

Labyrinthian? Too complex? Actually it's the other way around. Confining your notetaking and record keeping to specific pads or cards and tying all together by their sources— (2) references and (3) resources— does everything you want it to: provides information, sources, spinoff ideas, and additional biographical data all at hand and documented.

A writing schedule and tools

Figure out your publication date, subtract two or five months for the production phase, and you will know how many months you have to put words on paper. Then set a daily or regular quota, take the pledge, and get writing. Some measure their output in chapters (one a week, for example), in pages (2-5 a day), or in words (maybe 2,000-3,000). The important thing is to set a pace that can be maintained and stay at it, or ahead.

As for your writing tools, that is left to your imagination. But if you're going to self-publish and want to avail yourself of the marvels of desktop or electronic phototypesetting, at some point you will have to put those words in a computer. Why not start that way so you never have to make the transfer?

A personal note: I resisted computers like children fight spinach, for reasons about as sound. But one day of simple word processing and I was convinced. It was twice as fast as typing because of the editing facility, looked better, and could be sent to any other machine or typesetter. My volume of output has at least tripled, freeing me to do other things not related to writing— or more writing.

Some no less basic thoughts about editing and proofing

There are three levels of editing. The first you do as you write, by moving words around mentally and on paper. This should be kept to a minimum. Think in simple sentences, put them down, and go on to the next thought. That way you can finish the first draft while you are still living.

When the first draft is completed, you must then go through the text word-by-word and make each justify its existence. Seek the precise word. Clarity and accuracy are essential. If you can't make your copy read clearly and correctly, you must hire someone who can.

At this point, if a firm is publishing your work, you will send this final, self- (or helper-) edited draft for their further editing. If you are self-publishing, you must hire a good editor/proofreader. However good you are, don't do it yourself!

Where do you find editors and proofreaders? Some are listed in the *Literary Market Place* and your telephone book. Some advertise in writers' magazines. Check with your local writers' clubs or organizations. Consider faculty in the English and journalism departments at a local college. I've had good success with librarians. You can seek references (and going rates) from local publishers. Rates are also listed in the current Writer's Market.

When publishing with another firm, your final draft will be returned with proofreading marks. (If they don't send an explanation sheet, dictionaries usually decipher the symbols in the front or back section.) You will be asked to make changes, approve the changes suggested, or explain your disapproval and send the copy back for typesetting. After the galleys are typeset you will be asked once more to read them to find errors. This you should do yourself. It is your last chance to see what is going out under your name. Remember, though, that any other changes made at the galley stage can be costly and will usually be charged against your royalties, so edit and proof well before submitting the final draft.

When self-publishing, you will have another person edit and proof your copy, you will correct the text before sending it for typesetting, and you will have to read the galleys again word-for-word. Finally, after the galley copy has been pasted and is about to be sent to the printer, read it all a third time — and have the editor/proofreader do it too!

Illustrations

The illustrations most commonly found in books are photographs, charts, graphs, line drawings, and other artwork such as cartoons. Study other books like yours, then review the contents of your own book to see if illustrations are appropriate or needed.

If another firm will publish your book, share your thoughts with the editor and see whether you will be asked to provide illustrations or suggest examples or sources. To further explain, let's say that your book tells how to play *pelota de guante*. While researching, if you are to be involved with illustrations you will want to check and note the credit of every photo you see about this Andean sport and, if you are in Quito, you may want to take photos as well as get the name of local professional photographers that the publisher might later hire.

If you are publishing your own book, either you must provide illustrations or you must secure them. Precisely what you need, how they will be used, their approximate size, whether horizontal or vertical in shape, and the paper on which they will be printed must all be determined early. Even more important is whether they will be printed in black and white or color.

Photographer's Market is an excellent source for photos, photographers, and release information. Professional photographers at local stores, newspapers, and colleges add to the available pool of talent and information. For stock photos, also check the *Literary Market Place* and the *Stock Photo and Assignment Source Book* at your library.

As for drawings and graphics, local artists often serve quite well. Ask the local art club or league for names. Graphic artists and advertising firms are another source. Sometimes students of art, journalism, or computer graphics can be hired or will serve an internship working on your book. Local ads often draw herds of cartoonists.

Self-publishers involving others in the illustration of their books might well avail themselves of *Publishing Contracts* by Dan Poynter and Charles Kent (Para Publishing, P.O. Box 4232, Santa Barbara, CA 93140). These are sample agreements for publishers on disk. Of particular interest here are (18) Release for Photographs and Illustrations, (19) Illustration and Artwork Agreement, and (20) Agreement for Paste Up, Layout, and Book Design.

Copyright and your book

Specific, free information is available about copyright by calling the office of your senator or congressperson or by writing the Copyright Office, Library of Congress, Washington, DC 20559.

I'm not a lawyer so if you need legal advice in this area you should seek it. But there is little mystery to copyrighting your book.

One, you want to register the copyright after your book has been printed for each form in which it appears (cloth, paper, etc.) You will also want to contact the Library of Congress to get an LC catalog number well before you go to print: see the Poynter book for details. Both of these will be done for you if another publishes your text.

All the copyright does is prevent others from using the words (or charts, photos, etc.) as they appear. To do so they would need your permission. What you create is yours. That is, the words in the order in which an idea is expressed are yours. The idea, however, is anybody's. Others can restate that idea in their way, even similarly to yours. And they can use your words in other combinations.

Conversely, when you use others' words from copyrighted sources on your book's pages you need their permission. Or you must significantly restate their ideas. (Note that government printed material is almost never copyrighted and thus can be reused at will.) You will also need permission for illustrations, unless they were produced for you on a work-for-hire basis. But words said to you in interviews do not need written or stated permission as long as the person is aware that they will or may be used for publication. Nor is anything stated in public protected.

Since the words are yours, their use by other means are also protected. For example, the rights to articles or a script are, like the book rights, yours to give or sell to others.

Permission to quote letter

If you use a significant amount of information directly from another source, in the same words or nearly so, you will want to have permission to do so signed and in your possession before your book is typeset. (If another publisher is handling your book, they will have you get the permission to send to them.)

What is significant? I don't know and the courts aren't very clear. Titles have no copyright protection. Material written more than 110 years ago is almost certain to be in public domain. But as little as a word or two of a song or poem is significant given the total number of words. Several sentences or a paragraph or more from another's article or book most likely needs a permission release. When in doubt, give credit and get permission — or express the idea in different words or in a different way.

How do you get that permission? The same way that others will seek it when they want to quote your book. This fictitious example shows how a letter might look that I would receive requesting permission to use material from one of my books. It is very similar to another model in Herbert W. Bell's *How To Get Your Book Published* (Writer's Digest Books, 1985). Note that both segments are part of the same letter. You send back the second copy, signing the bottom section, when/if you grant permission.

DATE

Permissions Department
Communication Unlimited
P.O. Box 6405
Santa Maria, CA 93456

I am writing a trade book entitled Entrepreneurs and the New Age, to be published by Ajax Press. It will consist of approximately 220 pages and be priced at $14.95. I understand that the first printing will be 5,000 copies.

Identified below is material from one of your publications that I would like permission to include in my work, including any paperback, book club, braille, large type, and foreign language editions or recordings of the work that may be made throughout the world.

A duplicate copy of this letter and a self-addressed, stamped envelope is enclosed for your convenience in replying. If permission is granted, please sign and return one copy of the letter, indicating on it how you would like the credit line to read.

                                              Sincerely yours,

                                              Budding Editor

MATERIAL TO BE USED:

From Empire-Building by Writing and Speaking, by Gordon Burgett, the title and full list on pages 9-10 (paper and cloth editions), "Fifteen Steps to Empire-Building ... objective, means, and implementation."

Permission granted by _____
Date _____
Requested credit line:

EXAMPLE

Time to get to work, rearranging and researching and writing my million-dollar opus. Although doing that purely as an example gets tricky, otherwise we'll have two books in one. So I'll explain the process and show the key steps here. And leave out some items where, in fact, what you must do for your book isn't advanced much, if at all, by what I'd do for mine. A deal?

Recustomizing first

Remember the old purpose statement from Chapter 6?

> The purpose of this book is to share with principals ways by which they can serve their schools, families, and communities with love and lasting distinction while also leading balanced, challenging, full lives during and after principalship.

Time to bring that into much tighter focus, so I can see at every step whether my book is doing what I want. Here's my replacement (and final) purpose statement:

> The purpose of this book is to show principals how they can lead brighter, richer, happier lives during and after their principalship by focussing on five elements: their families, fun, fire (excitement, vigor, imagination), fortune, and their future.

With a new purpose statement comes a new restatement into a working question:

> How can principals, now and later, lead brighter, richer, happier lives, with emphasis on their families, fun, fire, fortune, and their future?

The secondary questions create the book's outline, which in turn dictates the purpose and thrust of the research.

A second look at the many books for principals in the library shows nothing aimed at answering the working question, though a closer look at their contents and bibliographies shows rare, tepid jabs into the revolutionary concept that principals are people too, with the hopes, dreams, and despair that other mortals know.

So I am going straight to the field to find principals who in fact lead the kinds of lives that others would want and would benefit from knowing about. I'm going to use what works for them, sometimes in their own words, other times drawing conclusions or using what they say and do as examples.

But I won't abandon the library altogether. In addition to using live examples, I will seek, in writing, information about how all professionals enrich their "non-professional" lives while and after they practice their profession, then I'll adapt those findings to principals.

An example of the latter would be what every steady wage earner should know and do about laying a base for a financially comfortable retirement. Then I'll adjust that to the principal's lot, reinforcing (and adding to) it through examples of what actual retired principals did. Or how others handle job stress or burnout and convert it into renewed energy and strength.

The illustrations were already mentioned: 20 cartoon-type drawings. When I get the book together in rough form I'll know where I want these injected, and will let my cousin know the themes so she can start on the choices.

The angle? That of an information gatherer and explainer, third person with some direct background as a principal (for our bio purposes here). It's not my story but the words of many principals and other experts from which the reader can select and use what makes the most sense and cents to him or her. All done objectively, though I subjectively pick what is included. It might not hurt to join the NASSP and NAESP, the two largest organizations for principals, if they have some affiliate category and that will both get me into meetings and the convention as well as give me access to the mailing list or membership directories.

Testimonials? Co-authorship? A foreword by some luminary? I'll ask the principals as I interview them if any name comes to mind that would, with its endorsement and name attached, give the book instant approval or sell thousands of additional copies. I doubt they will suggest such a name. After the book is out, I hope to get hundreds of principals writing rave letters, and I will naturally use those as quickly as I can on the promotional fliers. I will actually advance this a bit by showing the galley proofs (before the typeset copy is sent to the printer) to select principals, get their raves first, and put those on the initial flyer. But as things stand now the authorship will be mine, there will be no foreword by another person, and the book covers will be free of others' praise.

Tightly-Targeted Markets

Research: the library and the interviews

I will use the "one way to record information" technique at every step since it works, simplifies, and provides sources for all follow-up. But what will I put on my legal pads, how will I get it, and in what order?

The library work will come first since that will give me a solid base from which to ask questions to principals later. I'll find a good university library, search out the reference librarian, and ask for ten minutes of his/her precious time to guide me through the best fact-gathering process. I'll show my purpose statement and working question, tell the librarian what I've done (and not found) about the main topic in the library, and suggest that I'm thinking of backing into the subject by seeing what all professionals do to enrich their lives while practicing their profession. Then the killer questions: Is that the best approach? Can you suggest another way? How do I do it?

Sometimes librarians want to think about it and have you come back in an hour, a day, or next week. Great. I'll ask what I might do to profitably use my time in the interim. But when the reference librarian does suggest an approach, I'll follow it — using my own wisdom and intuition to expand or roam even wider or deeper.

Next come interviews, once I have a sense of the things that other, well balanced, fully living professionals do.

My book will be sold nationwide so I need examples that principals in every corner of the country can relate to. Which means a good mix of locations from which I will draw examples and quotations. Alas, my budget has $750 for research! What to do?

What kind of principals do I want to interview? Winners in school and out. Victors doing the kinds of things my book proposes, principals with their lives in full bloom and in order. Involved with their families, active, vigorous, prosperous, and planning for a complete life and a rich retirement.

I can find the best examples by mail. I'll prepare a one-page letter to send to selected superintendents explaining precisely what I'm seeking, the kinds of principals (practicing or retired) whom I'd like to interview, and ask if they might suggest several from their area, with addresses or phone numbers I could use for follow-up in the coming two to three weeks.

Then I'll get out a map, pick several dozen districts across the country (mixing elementary and secondary, rural and city, rich and poor), and send the letters near the time I'm ready to interview. At the same time I'll select six or eight districts within driving distance, call those superintendents to explain what I'm doing, tell them I'm sending a letter, and do it. (The call is to establish a closer bond since most of my in-depth personal interviews will be with nearby principals, given my budget.)

Most of my budget will go to the phone company. I'll follow up on all leads from the superintendents (sending them thank you letters later) by calling the principals indicated. Some will give me quotable material right over the phone. (Best if you have a recording device and ask, after the conversation is over, if it's okay to use the comments in the book. You can use them whether or not they give permission; almost none will say no.)

Some will want to put their thoughts on paper. That's all the better since I can direct specific questions to them, then follow up again, later, for details by phone. I expect that most of my best material will come this way.

If there's money available and I want a tax-deductible trip, I can head off in some direction and do some in-depth personal interviews with the selected principals in that area. Or I can gather several together in a round table setting and simply turn on the tape recorder, later plucking from the comments those that I can use!

Incidentally, must I pay them for their words or ideas? Heavens no, other than in fame by having their names and comments in print forever. I will send two copies of the book to each participant when it's published, with a second thank you note. The first note is sent the day after the interview.

The purpose of all this? To create a pool of interesting, live dialog for my book that will bring the ideas and message directly home to the buyer. A rich blend of fact, from books, and commentary, from life, is like blending two prime coffees: it gets bought. That's my purpose.

A writing schedule and tools

Rather than pinpoint the precise number of words or hours per day, I expect to have this book ready to distribute in five months. That figures two weeks for basic library research, about 12 hours a week; a few days getting my letters and calls to the superintendents; two weeks writing basic copy for the book from library information, as I continue to use the library, about 10 hours a week; three weeks on the phone and with follow-up letters to the principals suggested by superintendents; a week getting the copy and the interviews integrated; a week of personal interviews with nearby principals, to expand the material already at hand and to fill in the gaps; one month to write the main draft; about 15 days to get it edited and prepare the final manuscript; five days to code it for electronic phototypesetting, send it, receive back the galleys, proof them, and insert corrections; four days to paste the final galleys and prepare the boards, with illustrations and cover, for the printer, and some 30 days for the book to get printed and returned.

As for tools, I go right to my computer and plan to use the same machine, with a modem, to send the copy for phototypesetting. (Or I can mail the disks.) I need a decent printer to write letters to the superintendents and principals. Later I will need a waxer or a large bottle of rubber cement, a straightedge, a table, some non-photo blue pencils, some tape, and scissors for the pasteups. That's it. With a more advanced computer and software I could even send the pages to the phototypesetter prepasted, but what would I do with those extra four days?

Editing and proofing

The editing is no problem. I don't worry about it at all. I know what I mean while I write my basic copy. It's only important for the letters sent to others, so if I had any question here I'd ask the same proofreader who will read my copy later to do the same for the letters.

Once I have the basic copy in the computer, I run it through the spellcheck. That will pick up most of the inverted letters or real inventions, but it won't find misspellings if they are in fact another word, like "too" for "to." And it won't tell me where the words are right but they don't mean anything — or six unintended things at once.

So I need an editor/proofreader, which I have found. She gets the copy in neat, printout fashion, double-spaced, with my full encouragement to challenge everything and correct all grammar, spelling, and improper word use. The copy returns days or weeks later amply commented upon. Which I must review item-by-item, moving words around, clarifying, sometimes rejecting the advice (at peril). I enter all changes into the computer; the result is a much clearer, quicker, and correct manuscript.

She also gets paid the day I pick up the last correction. Invaluable aid that deserves the quickest compensation.

Copyright and permission to quote

After the book is out I will go through the copyrighting process, but when I typeset copy I include the copyright symbol, the letter "c" in a circle, followed by the date and my name on the page behind the title.

If I use a block of somebody else's words, I will send a "Permission to Quote" letter well before the date my copy gets set, so I know that I can use the material. Otherwise I run a risk of that person or their publisher pressing a suit against me and an injunction against the release or sale of my book, or worse. Usually, though, I avoid quoting directly in this fashion, restating and referring to the original source. That does not need others' permission.

Nor do I need permission to include the quotes from the principals as long as I took notes or recorded them on tape, used the quote as said, and repeat the words in the spirit and context for which they were sought. I'm presuming that each principal understood that I was gathering information for a book, which I mentioned each time that we spoke or in the letter sent.

13 PRODUCING THE BOOK - OR HAVING IT PRODUCED

It's one thing to write a book, it's another and a far more complex thing to produce a book that you would want to show to colleagues, sell to peers, and stake a reputation on.

On the surface, converting prose into serif text on numbered pages with captioned illustrations and chapter headings, a table of contents and index, the ISBN number secured and correctly placed, four colors on the cover (or two with screening, if possible), errorless and tasteful and reeking of professionalism, is enough to drop novices to their knees begging a New York house to keep at least 90% to "do it right"!

Even worse, it is about as confusing as it seems. And yet what you are building — the term is right — is, for all its stairwells and towers, no more complex than rolling up your sleeves and following steps, one by one, in a sensible order, doing personally what you can and letting a professional do the rest.

Fortunately, you've had the product in your hand since first grade. A book is a book. Your task is to convert your knowledge into a peculiar kind of book eagerly sought by your targeted market. Still, it has a cover, pages, words, illustrations, and an order.

And you have another advantage: there are several excellent texts that will take you through the process, step-by-step. They are so good there is no reason for me to say inadequately in one chapter what needs many hundreds of pages to do right. So I will limit myself here to providing a list of particularly useful books, plus add some comments and a chart. The rest I leave to other books that explain book production.

Where to find help about self-publishing

I used two books to help me convert my ideas into publications. Since my books were not tightly targeted, but for the general writing and speaking public, these books were triply helpful: in preparation, production, and promotion.

Dan Poynter's *The Self-Publishing Manual* has been repeatedly mentioned on these pages. I used the 1979 version, and have continued to consult each of the four revised printings for the newest names and addresses of services in the field. The book is chuck full of facts, guides, a production calendar, and examples.

As useful was the earlier version of Tom and Marilyn Ross's book on this topic. Better yet is their 1986 Writer's Digest up-date called *The Complete Guide to Self-Publishing*. What distinguishes these books is the clarity of example and the depth of how-to information.

Where the TCE approach differs

The Poynter and Ross books discuss self-publishing in the conventional sense and are excellent for general, small publishers, who are numerically in the vast majority today.

Self-Publishing to Tightly-Targeted Markets suggests that there is a different way of publishing that can make books that are otherwise probably too marginal for conventional preparation and marketing nonetheless highly successful and profitable. This book suggests that way, and provides both framework and guidelines for the self-publisher serving a tightly-targeted market. The major difference is in the order in which things are done and how the specific needs of a particular buying audience are met.

Poynter and Ross suggest that the self-publisher with a general book (1) writes (or has another write) the book, (2) produces the book, and (3) sells the book, pretty much in that order.

I propose that the self-publisher to a tightly-targeted market (1) finds the target market first, defines what that market needs to read and couldn't resist buying if it were available, and identifies the selling requisites, then (2) writes (or has written) the book so it is in fact deservedly irresistible, and finally (3) produces that irresistibility for all to see. The actual selling of that book (4) is a simple extension of the first three.

Which means that when Poynter and Ross discuss preparation and promotion, what they say, all useful and applicable in its own context, must be sifted and weighed as to its value and order in the TCE process.

Yet what they say about production works fine for the tightly-targeted book. So I send you their way to learn how to produce your book, to absorb and follow and adapt, to turn out your own masterpiece, one that meets every requisite of your hungry market.

What is production?

Production is everything from taking the words on the final, corrected manuscript to turning out a finished book ready to sell. That includes type selection and setting, cover choice and binding, book design, bidding, layout, paper preference, illustrations, printing, and more.

Who should do what?

Few folks are universally gifted, and of those even fewer have the time or interest to do all aspects of book production well.

What you can probably do better than others is the targeting, research, writing, general production coordination, pasteup, sales marketing, promotion, and fulfillment. If not, move those items where you are deficient, disinterested, or short of time to the next paragraph.

You might seriously consider hiring others for the editing and proofreading, book design, cover design and artwork preparation, printing, and perhaps the flyer artwork.

It isn't easy to find such artisans with book preparation experience. The *Literary Market Place* is a place to start. Check other publishers. See if there are regional publishing associations or contact the Publishers Marketing Association (PMA), at 2401 Pacific Coast Highway, #206, Hermosa Beach, CA 90254, or COSMEP, at P.O. Box 703, San Francisco, CA 94101 for any source guidance they might offer. The telephone book is a first guide. Sometimes you can swap services with other self-publishers if you are proficient where the other is not.

A supplementary flow chart

While other books will show you what you need to know about book production, a simple flow chart might give your action better cohesion and direction. That is the purpose of this chart:

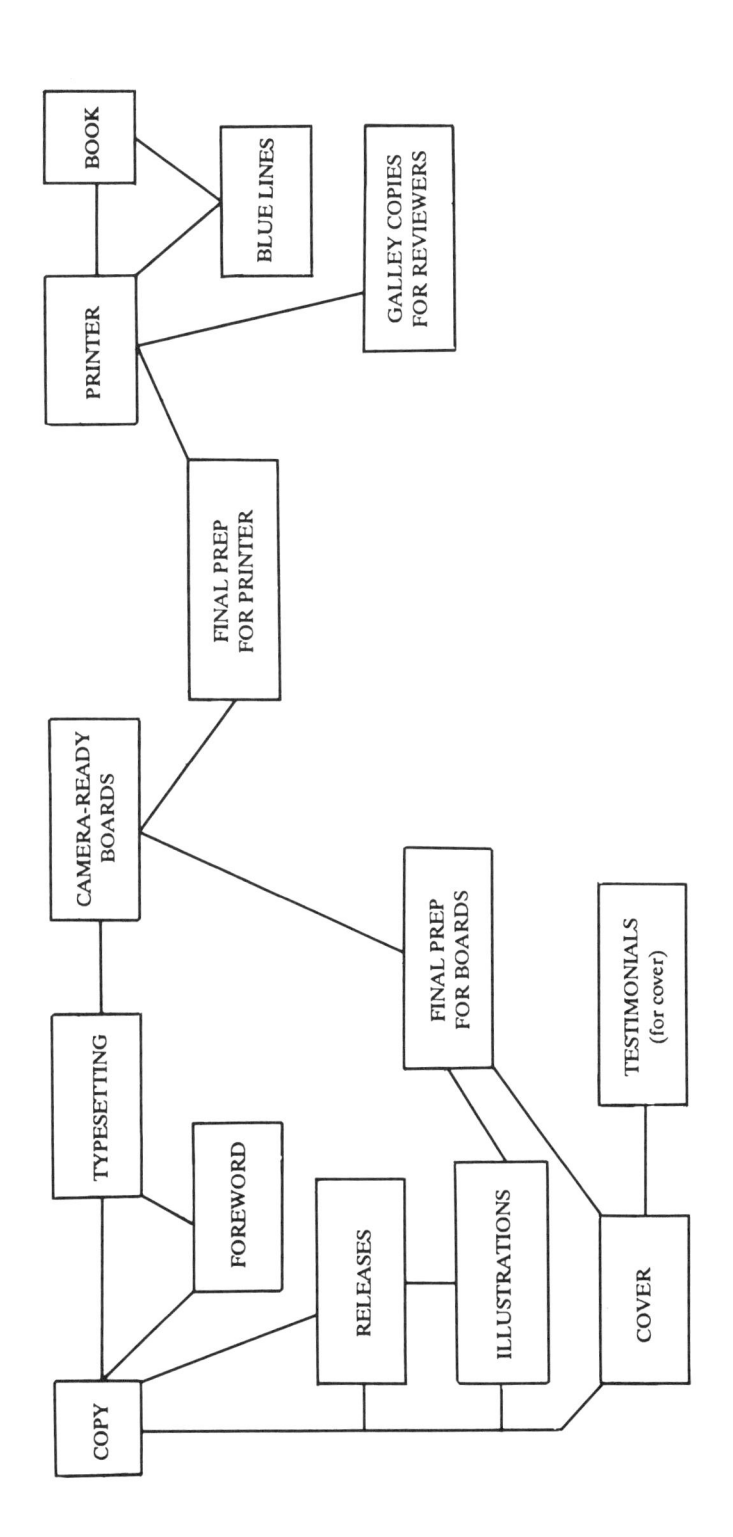

Tightly-Targeted Markets

In summary, while writing the book, you must consider other production needs. Some texts require illustrations, which must be produced or bought. If you are using others' words or illustrations, you must also secure releases. And somewhere early on, the cover art must be done and printers must be bid.

Two kinds of testimonials help sell books to tightly-targeted (and most other) markets: short, laudatory comments on the cover(s) and a foreword. They too must be secured before the cover artwork is finalized or the book is typeset.

Typesetting is next, which often means coding the computer text. It's prudent to complete the book design before setting the copy! Final text and illustrations are gathered, and all are pasted (or computer-plotted) on camera-ready boards. Sometimes copies of the galley proofs are made at this point to send to book reviewers.

The camera-ready boards and the final cover artwork are sent to the printer, who returns blue line copies before the actual printing. If approved, printing and shipping complete the production phase.

Some final thoughts about the above steps

(1) **Typesetting**. What your market needs and expects will dictate here. There are five ways copy is usually prepared for the boards:

- (a) *typewritten*. Looks amateurish, detracts from contents and your professionalism.
- (b) *proportional type/computer*. Probably unacceptable. Very difficult to do underlining and boldface well.
- (c) *electronic phototypesetting*. The best for most books. Can be reasonable and quick; available in a wide variety of fonts. Least expensive if you code on your computer, then send by modem or disk.
- (d) *laser printing*. Varies in quality from poor to excellent. Too expensive to buy machinery for one book. Consider (c) first.
- (e) *old fashioned typesetting*. Very expensive. Go to (C) or to (d).

(2) **Book Design and Camera-Ready Boards**. Find other books in your market, or elsewhere, that you want your book to look like. What kind and size of type? How big will the book be? Where will the numbers go? How will the chapters headings and sub-headings look?

Will you use footnotes? There must be some consistent rationale. Either design it or get someone else to do so. Must work for your market.

An excellent book for pasteup, to prepare your camera-ready boards, is Walter Graham's *Complete Guide to Pasteup* (3rd edition, P.O. Box 369, Omaha, NE 68101). Graham shows you how to mark the boards properly, adhere the copy, and tie in the illustrations. Once the boards are pasted, prepare the index. All go to the printer — very well packaged.

(3) **Printers**. Some time early in the process prepare a master bid and send it to the most likely short-run printers. Use the *Literary Market Place* for the most recent list. John Kremer's current *Directory of Short-Run Printers* can also be helpful: Ad-Lib Publications, P.O. Box 1102, Fairfield, IA 52556.

If printers are new to you, a superb book demystifies these odd souls and shows you what they can do to make your book shout quality and professionalism. Read *Getting It Printed: How to Work With Printers and Graphic Arts Services to Assure Quality, Stay on Schedule, and Control Costs* by Mark Beach, Steve Shepro, and Ken Russon (Coast to Coast Books, 2934 Northeast 16th Avenue, Portland, OR 97212).

Don't worry about bidding too early. If you bid on 204 pages and 50-pound paper and later want 220 pages and 60-pound, they will adjust the cost. Just send the same numbers to every printer in the first bid so you can compare. When you pick a winner, check recent customers to see if the printer met the quality and promised delivery date. If so, set up final dates for board/cover delivery, blue lines, and anything else pending.

(4) **Releases**. If you absolutely need or want to use something requiring are lease, get it as soon as possible. Releases should be in hand before the final copy is set. Or you can set the copy two ways: with the original and without, reworded or simply deleted in case it doesn't arrive by the day the copy goes to the printer.

(5) **Illustrations**. These depend on three things: (1) how vital they are to the text, (2) if there is sufficient space, and (3) the kind of paper and press used. The first is the most important: are they a must to this market? If so, find space. But be certain that you make clear to each printer what you plan to include and the paper you will use. If high quality resolution is required, ask to see examples of what was done with similar work in the past. No surprises here.

(6) **Cover.** How it will be bought is most important, and how the other books to your market are sold. If your buyers only buy cloth (hard cover), your book will be covered in cloth! But if you want to save buyers money and that is important, a trade paperback is what you need.

Whether you need two, three, or four colors in your cover artwork is largely determined by where it will be bought. For bookstores, an eyecatcher of many colors. If sold through a flyer, sharp, distinct colors that photograph and reproduce well in print are mandatory. Often TCE books meet both criteria. But avoid putting reds and blacks next to each other: both are black to the b/w camera!

(7) **Binding.** Do what other books to your market do, unless there is some compelling reason. If your book is a cookbook or should lay flat to be read (like a typing textbook), use some comb for binding.

(8) **Blue Lines.** This is the last chance to see the book exactly as it will appear in print. Go over it very closely. Making changes at this stage costs time and money and can often result in a delayed printing, so much more attention should be paid to the final galleys before they are pasted down. Blue lines are important to see if the printer inserted the right photos in the right places in the right way. Do you need blue lines? Prudence says yes. But they raise the cost. If you are really concerned about the opening sections of the book, get blue lines for the first 32 pages.

(9) **Book.** Some additional thoughts:

(a) If you want part of the books to go elsewhere after printing and the printer is closer, have them sent directly to that buyer or destination, with the bill sent to you (or them).
(b) Consider shrinkwrapping each book. Costs 6-12 cents but provides excellent shipping protection against moisture and scuffing. If sold in bulk, consider having four or five wrapped per package.
(c) Make certain the boxes are well padded and tightly packed at the printers, and check the whole shipment closely when it arrives, breaking into boxes at random to see how they travelled.
(d) Stipulate that every box should be marked clearly: title, paper or cloth, and box weight — for inventory control later.

EXAMPLE

How would I produce this book if I were like you, a newcomer who (if you are like me) has trouble mixing paint or drawing a straight line? By the numbers, carefully, and with one overriding purpose in mind, to turn out a book that looks so good, so "right" for my market, that those in it would feel naked not having my masterpiece under their arm.

By the numbers means by following, step-by-step, what Poynter or Ross suggest. Alas, since their suggestions are explicit I will only highlight what I would do, letting them flesh out the action and timing in their how-to texts. (You'll also get the advantage of my having done just this for six earlier books. And you can look at the pages in hand to see if I follow my own advice in book seven!)

Setting up my company

There's a hidden benefit from publishing my own book. I become the president of the company that makes and sells it! I also become the janitor, treasurer, and general factotum. My company then needs a presence: a name, stationery, an address, a bank account, and some numbers that give it legitimacy in the publishing world, called the ISBN and LC numbers.

To open a bank account the company must bear my name, only, or I must complete and file a fictitious business statement at the county courthouse, plus have a legal notice in print a required number of times. Since I've chosen the name Bassman-Willer Press for this example, it's off to court I go. Cost: about $50 total.

Since I plan to sell my books, the state tax board must issue me a resale number. I apply, fill in the forms, and set up simple income and order-filling procedures so I can account for and pay the Governor his due. Then I need a city business license: another $12. I'd rather not break my home mail carrier's back delivering truckloads of orders so I rent a a post office box for an additional $39. And I need decent looking stationery, some invoices, and perhaps a small number of business cards, which I buy from NEBS for about $75 total.

Off go letters to R.R. Bowker and Company about the ISBN number and to the CIP Office of the Library of Congress about that number, which I will follow up on later. The instructions they send me are explicit.

All that remains is to dedicate a room to the company work, find a large storage place in the garage for the certain arrival of boxes of books, hook up the computer and telephone, and remind the children that as president of the company I'm no longer to be held in the same questionable regard that they show when I am simply the author of the book. In other words, if they straighten up I, as president and treasurer, may later let them earn some good hard cash when it comes time to wrap, seal, and ship.

Finding experts who do the real book production

I wrote the book, I know what my market buys, I have a solid concept of what I want (and don't want) on my pages, and I am eager to do the linking that will turn out a solid product. But I need experts to do most of the actual work.

I need a **printer** who will give me precisely what I want inexpensively and on time. We took care of that in Chapter 10, except that I need to know two more things: does he keep his promises and how do other books appear after they come off that firm's press? So I call my top choice and ask for names of recent customers with books like mine, and I then call each of them to see if that printer delivers what's promised and on time. If I'm satisfied, I call the same printer again and ask to see a copy of a recent book that has the same type of cover and photos or illustrations in it. If that looks acceptable, I arrange a date for my camera-ready copy to be sent. All else is directed at meeting that date.

The second expert is a **typesetter**. I've already narrowed my hunt to three, so here I do the same: get the names of recent book customers to call. From their response and my own gut feeling, I pick one. Then I ask to see an example of a book or two they have set. Satisfied, we set a date for consultation to establish a coding format.

To that meeting I bring a design I have in mind for my book. It will probably be a combination of things I see in other books, each example of which I copy, all put into a sensible order. From the examples and my simple design the typesetter can determine the kind and size of type, the leading, the chapter headings, and all of the unique style items I want on my pages. I'm going to listen closely to his or her suggestions too, for some styles may look inviting on one page but would exhaust a reader for a full book. My ideas are starters. From them and the typesetter's experience we will devise a coding format, which I will insert in the final copy so the disks, when delivered, will tell the typesetter's machinery how to produce galleys exactly like I want.

I plan to have my final, coded copy to the typesetter two weeks before the camera-ready copy is due at the printer, based on the turnover time of 36 hours given to me by the typesetter — with corrections, if any, in 12 hours or less.

The **cover artist** gives me the most concern because the final cover boards must be completed a week before I send all of the boards to the printer. Concern because artists are, well, artists. Again, I have three choices. I now have a date, so when I visit each of the three I emphasize as strongly as I can my concern about that date — which I move one week earlier, just in case!

I tell each of the artists roughly what I have in mind for a cover, remind them that the ISBN number must be included (giving the person the number), then ask for their thoughts. Is the resulting idea possible? Can it be done prior to the date? In what order will the work be done? How quickly will I get to see the preliminary sketch or design? How much will that cost? How much will the total job cost? And for whom have you prepared book covers: name, phone, how long ago?

The same verifications before I select one for the project. I try to get the preliminary sketch or design done quickly, close to its final form. That is the first half of the agreement. If I like it and want to continue, the second half is the preparation of the cover boards. If I don't, I still have time to turn to the second artist and begin again.

So I select, get the prelims moving, and hope.

No problem with my **illustrator**. My cousin is hopping with excitement so I set some hours aside now and pick out the elements of the text that lend themselves to humorous cartoon-like drawings. I draw up a master list for both of us, explain in several sentences what each segment is about (noting the actual manuscript page location for layout purposes later), suggest any humorous ideas that come to my mind, and sit down for an overview session with her.

I tell her about my audience — principals — and that I want the illustrations to bring a smile, be in good taste, and be a certain size. I plan to leave islands in the text in the right and left margins (depending on whether it is an even- or odd-numbered page) by indenting the copy where illustrations appear. This I have worked out with the typesetter so her drawings must be made or reduced to specific dimensions.

Finally, we work out a schedule for sketches, then the final work.

Getting it all together

I simply follow the flow chart at this point, calling the cover artist and the illustrator every few weeks both to inquire and to offer encouragement. Then I code the final, proofed copy, take both disks over to be typeset, read the galleys word-for-word, and have any corrections reset quickly.

The final illustrations are now in my possession, so they and the typeset copy are laid out and pasted on the boards. A photocopy of the boards is made and given to the proofreader for one last, final read-through. I read the original with the same attention, then prepare an index now that the copy is finally tied down to specific text pages. The proofreader returns the board corrections and then looks over the index for spelling and other errors.

In the meantime, the cover boards arrive! All is joined together, carefully packaged, and sent to arrive at the printer several days in advance. I call the contact person when it is sent and two days later to confirm its arrival. If bluelines are being returned, I look at those immediately and call back within hours, giving the go-ahead. (On the rare chance that something is amiss, I can handle that by phone too. Speed is essential here.)

When the book is in the printing phase, I call weekly to monitor its progress. And soon enough, usually within a day or two of the promised delivery, a truck backs up and with a depressing lack of nobility a pallet or two of book boxes is lowered. Unsold books that keep the car in the elements until the stacks can be reduced. Promotion follows— quickly!

14 PROMOTING AND SELLING THE BOOK

Done right, you promote and sell a TCE book from the moment you conceptualize it until the last copy leaves your warehouse or garage. The actual exchange of money for bound volumes is the natural conclusion of developing a product for a buyer that he/she wants and perceives as being the solution to a problem or a need.

How you let the buyer know that this invaluable object exists and can be bought is the focus of this chapter.

First, let me review the standard approach to selling a book. You will use some of those means. More important, you must know how and why the TCE approach differs.

Then I will discuss how to use those standard promotional tools to increase your book sales. Knowing how to prepare your flyer, then how to distribute it is critical. Finally, assuming that all this promotional whirl creates sales, you'll need some ideas about filling orders, called "fulfillment" in the trade.

The standard approach to selling a book

The standard approach presumes that most books will be sold through bookstores, and that widespread interest can be created through general newspaper reviews, radio and TV talk shows, and other public means of advertising. Secondarily, it focusses on the library market, again encouraging review by major library magazines as a way to bring the book to the attention of the acquisition librarian. Also encouraged is direct mailing to book reviewers, bookstores, and librarians.

Since bookstores and libraries often buy through their own distributors or fulfillment sources, it behooves a publisher to court those intermediates to get them both to handle and "push" the book.

Alas, almost all of this approach directly conflicts with the TCE method because success in the latter comes from having identified a specific market at the outset, customized your book to meet its very needs, and then

Tightly-Targeted Markets

expanded from that base. Which means that only a small percentage of the public is likely to buy your book, although a high percentage of that fraction will. So a selling campaign that depends upon the book being selected by the public at large would be, for you, excessively expensive for too small a yield.

More specifically, if your targeted market is bakers or ice fishermen or criminal lawyers it is unlikely that either general bookstores or libraries will be very interested in stocking or displaying your wares. Yet there is always the possibility that if your book is slanted in such a way that both its targeted market and the broader populace might find areas of common interest, at least libraries and perhaps bookstores may wish to add your book to their offerings. So some of these standard selling means might be selectively pursued. First, though, concentrate on getting your book in the hands of your targeted market. They are eager to devour its pages. That will fill your purse.

Using standard promotional tools for a TCE book

To sell a TCE book massively, fliers work best. One of every four books is sold by mail, and the tighter yours is marketed and the better your flyer, the better your chances are of earning $50,000+ this way. Best yet, the responses are fast: a reliable figure finds half of those who will respond doing so in four weeks, 98% in 13. Still, anything that informs your targeted market of the book's existence and desirability and makes it available for purchase should be investigated and probably pursued.

So let's quickly look at the standard promotional tools first, then discuss the flyer later, in greater detail. Some of the standard promotional means are more important to TCE sales than others. Let's discuss them in a rough, descending order of importance.

Testimonials, for starters. In every field there are people whose opinion others value. You want their opinions in your book, on its back cover, or in your flyer. There are two times when that is best sought. One, when the book is in the drafting stage. You might ask people to technically or critically review a chapter or two. Ask for a general testimonial at the same time. The second time is from the galley proofs or when the book is on the boards (before being sent to the printer); you can send a copy and ask for a short testimonial. Not all will say yes, some will want to wait until later, some will never reply — but, surprisingly, many will send you the blessed affirmation.

Do testimonials sell books? You bet. They help get better book reviews too. Another valuable kind of testimonial comes from satisfied buyers. These are usually letters. In all cases you should get the words in writing and ask for permission to use those words promotionally. It's also best to use the person's full name (rather than initials), occupation, and (if possible or relevant), age, and city of residence.

Testimonials are particularly valuable for TCE books. In tightly-targeted markets the sphere of acquaintances is usually smaller, the luminaries better known, and anybody else in the profession or field recommending the book can catapult it into a much better selling position.

Book reviews are even more valuable, if they are positive and appear in key magazines or journals read by your targeted market. They can result in many thousands of book sales. The key here is positioning. Brain surgeons or lepidopterists, for example, aren't likely to read and rush out to buy a book in their field that is reviewed in the *National Enquirer*. But in their own technical journals, yes. That's where they expect to find such reviews. Good words by a peer on the right pages make all the difference.

Poynter and Ross will tell you how to get books reviewed. They will also tell you how to get your book listed in the major directories: *Books in Print*, the Library of Congress indexes, *Publishers Weekly*, and library journals (if library sales are a possibility).

Other than a favorable book review, the most important standard promotional tool is an **article** in those selected publications most read by your targeted market. An article you write from, or relate to, the information discussed in your book. It can be a direct excerpt. Usually it will be part or all of a chapter reworded for magazine use. The material is yours to use; you can update it, add details magazine readers want to know, insert quotes culled for the article only, or expand the text to more closely fit readers' needs. Very important: your byline (or in the article itself, the details probably footnoted) should include the information that the material comes from your book, with its full title, publication date, and (hopefully) your address and the purchase price.

When a magazine or journal pays for articles, you win twice! Others will use the article and consider the plug your payment. Don't quibble: just being on those pages is worth gold — if the article is good! Two books take you through the how-to steps here: *How To Sell 75% of Your Freelance Writing* and *Query Letters/Cover Letters: How They Sell Your Writing*.

Book clubs are ideal ways to get widespread publicity and approval all at once, though *per se* they are not very lucrative. Most fields have their own book clubs, as the *Literary Market Place* indicates. They should be approached when the book is in the rough draft to galley stages since the club will want to buy the text as it is printed, usually paying the per unit production cost plus 10% of the sale rate at which it will sell the book to its members. With a significant order this can pay for all of your printing, their copies and yours, so that your sole expense would be the promotional cost of your copies. The rest is profit. The bonus? You print in big letters on every book: _____ BOOK CLUB TOP CHOICE (or whatever is appropriate)!

Card decks are often sent to specific markets and your book might well be promoted on such a card. Again, the Standard Rate and Data Services publications list card deck firms by markets served.

If your targeted market attends a convention or regional gatherings, a **display booth** might be considered. Not only could a giant reproduction of the book cover be shown, the actual book itself would be at hand to be touched and reviewed, and fliers could be given to every passer-by.

The best of all worlds would be for a firm to use your book as a **premium**, buying it in lot from you and distributing it to some or all of your target market. That requires a promotion of a different sort, to interest firms in your product as a premium. Poynter touches this.

You might distribute your fliers as part of a larger mailing, perhaps with other, similar books or even other products of direct interest to the target market. Seek the most prestigious group dealing with your target market and suggest an **insert**. You can shine by having your book promoted in a flyer inserted, say, in a magazine. That also sells books! Check the same SRDS publication that discusses card decks for information about insert programs.

Sometimes **display advertising** in journals and newsletters that serve your target market is worth the cost. (Place your own ad through a second company name and save the 15% commission; pay in cash and save 2% more.) Before that, as the book is being printed, send press releases to any publication that might be remotely interested whether or not you plan to advertise in them later. The release should describe the book's contents and you as its author.

Classified ads might also work. If your targeted market turns to specific classifieds, put an ad where they look. Don't list it under "book" unless they are accustomed to seeking items by that title. Better to list by topic. Nor should you mention the price, which is too high to justify in so few words. Get people to seek more information. Your response will include an irresistible flyer about your book, plus anything you offered to get them to write. (You also have their names for your mailing list whether they buy or not.) How do you get them to respond? Offer a teaser: "Ten ways to ... " Ten ways they need to know. Ten ways that lead to your book, which is the best way to do what the teaser suggests — or includes more information about all or some of the ten ways on its pages. Cut your costs further by requesting a self-addressed, stamped envelope to receive the information sought.

Speeches or **seminars** are seldom thought of as promotional tools, but they are exceptionally effective ways to sell your book. Not only can you make it available after the presentation (better yet, have the sponsor buy enough copies to give one free to every participant), the fact that you are speaking about the subject shows your expertise for having written about it. (Which is ironic since you often get the bookings because you did write about it!)

Radio and **TV** may help, if your target market watches or listens and you don't have to water down the subject too much to explain it to the average audience, thus making your knowledge and the book's content appear too elementary.

Are there **catalogs** serving your targeted market? Is your book included? Are there **commissioned reps** who sell to your most likely buyers? Are they selling your book? Does your targeted market have an **association** or trade group? Does it sell products? Yours? Does it sell your book in its bookstore? You must put the same sharp skills you used in writing your book to seeing how those in your target market find out about and buy books. Promotional and selling possibilities abound. Make every one of them tools for putting your words before the right eyes — at your price!

Anything that displays your expertise in the subject that your book is about should help sell more books. Yet you will sell many more books much faster to that market if they are aware of the book's existence beforehand. The best way to do that in your case is to begin with a flyer.

Preparing your flyer

Earlier you identified what must appear on this flyer: the benefits, the needs the book would meet, why a book was needed, and so on. You may have actually designed a dummy flyer.

Now review that material from Chapter 9, and the information sheet you sent to test the market in Chapter 11, and do the following:

(1) Make the content changes necessary to describe your actual book and its benefits. Study your target and secondary markets closely. Will the same flyer work for all? Do you need different fliers or approaches for different segments? How must they differ for each?

(2) Study closely every aspect of as many other fliers to your primary market as you can get. This is your competition, if not to sell a book at least to draw money from your market. How professional do they look? Are they typeset? How many colors? Expensive paper? Are they stamped or do they bear an indicia? Include a mail-back envelope? Postage paid? Contain artwork and illustrations? Such details can save you much and earn you more.

(3) Convert the benefits and needs into copy that will best appeal to your primary market. Determine the illustrations and artwork needed to produce a competitive flyer.

(4) If you need a graphic artist to design and produce your flyer, select the best available within your budget. (Where do you find one? Ask other publishers for recommendations, check the telephone directory, consider a student in graphic arts as an intern to create your flyer under faculty supervision.) Look at other work that person has designed for your target market or about books. Share the information you have gathered, set a working and verification schedule, and let that person work.

(5) If you design and produce your own flyer, go to it. Most book fliers include a photo of the book, its table of contents, something of your expertise or the expertise of others cited, a money-back guarantee, testimonials, and selling copy.

(6) Discuss your final design, paper, and how to best use the illustrations with a printer who produces in the volume range you need. Determine a kind of paper, the weight, and how the illustrations will be reproduced. From that information prepare a bid for that and several other printers. Select one printer and emphasize the need for the fliers on the promised date. Have the fliers printed.

Distributing the flyer

Now that you have the flyer planned or actually in hand, you must figure out the most effective yet least expensive way to put that flyer in the hands of your targeted market. You must learn about direct mail.

Books are written about direct mail. This isn't one of them. I will remind you here of the key steps plus some critical concerns. Just know that using the mail as a selling means is expensive, risky, and somewhat uncontrollable. But it can also bring you the best results fastest by getting your message precisely where you want it to go. For the TCE concept it is simply the very best primary means of promotion.

The two most important elements are the mailing list and the mailer.

Mailing List: You are already aware of accessible mailing lists to your targeted market, but if there are several, other considerations come into play: their availability (quantity and delivery date), cost, method of addressing, frequency of cleaning, source, date compiled, discount if placed through your in-house brokerage, and restrictions.

(1) Ask each list broker for particulars about their list. The SRDS mailing list publication already contains much of this information. You probably want a list that is current and just cleaned available in a few days on Cheshire labels, 4-up. An active list compiled from products or services bought is better than one compiled from directories or otherwise indirectly gathered. Best if the cost is low, the list can be ordered in installments (Nth selections non-repeating), and you can take the discount (deduct the commission).

(2) Determine when you will mail and how many names you will send at a time. Will you test a sampling first? What is the minimum number the list broker will let you test? Or will you mail to geographic sections? Will you mail twice to the same list, renting at a considerable reduction those second names with the first? Will you send different fliers to different levels of the list? All of this should be planned before you order lists.

(3) Order the best list or lists available.

Mailing: The question is whether you will do this yourself or will use a mailing house to coordinate all of the steps. I have found that for up to 1,000 I can save money by applying pressure-sensitive labels and handling our own bulk mailing in-house. But beyond that it is more economical to use a mailing house. Naturally you will want to check the rates of all the local houses. (You can find them listed in the telephone directory, by asking others who use direct mailing, or by calling the local Chamber of Commerce.)

(1) After selecting the house you will use, let them see your mailer early in the process. At issue are its size, weight, open space for the address, folding, and use of indicia or a stamp.

(2) In some states (like California) if the printing is delivered directly to the mailing house it is exempt from state tax. Check that and act accordingly.

(3) Cheshire labels are the most economical so work out the specifics with the house before ordering: coding, dimensions, number of labels across — anything unusual that you should tell the list broker.

You can have the lists sent directly to the mailer or to you, to deliver to the mailer.

(4) In fact, you can have the mailer order the lists for you. However, the mailer will then receive the commission. The advantage? If the wrong list is sent, or sent incorrectly, and you gave the mailing house the right information (in writing), they must correct the problem. And they have the clout to do it faster and better.

(5) If you use a bulk rate indicia instead of stamps, you can usually use that of the mailing house and save the $50 annual fee.

(6) The major problem with mailers: getting your items sent the day you want them to go. This requires coordination between you, the printer, the list provider, and the mailing house. Let them suggest the best times so they will perform as you wish.

Some tips about mailing those bought books: fulfillment

Once you have a flyer and the means to mail it, all that is left is to take the plunge, keep yourself busy for the next few days, then tend to the results. Which means fulfillment: getting those books back to the buyers as quickly as you can in first-rate condition, with a flyer, of course, that tells about other, related products and services you also offer!

Setting up a shipping department is the inevitable result of publishing a fast-selling book. Yet it needn't be a major headache nor entail extraordinary expenses. Simply set aside a large table, put the necessary items nearby, and either assign the task to some lucky employee or hire a part-timer to perform this function. It is ideal for your kids, somebody else's kids, or seniors. But they must be responsible and attentive; frequent praise and small raises work well here. Whoever does the job may need a car with a trunk to cart packages to the post office. The load is heaviest after you send your mailings and diminishes rather quickly between promotions. What follows are some quick tips that should save time and cost. More in Poynter and Ross.

(1) You need a mailing address so buyers can reach you. An office or P.O. Box are best at first since the post office may refuse to deliver to your home if the response is too large. Check with your Postmaster.

(2) The books must be wrapped well to reach buyers in good condition. We use Tyvek reinforced envelopes for regular customers and Jiffy bags or well padded boxes for bookstores or others who will resell the goods. An invoice is inserted for the resales, while fliers plus any receipts (for credit card purchases) go into the customer package. Both are then sealed securely and taped. A company address label goes on top. We buy Tyveks from Quill (100 S. Schelter Road, Lincolnshire, IL 60197) and Jiffy bags locally from a paper wholesaler; we use our book boxes and some from behind the liquor store to send out quantity purchases, and buy labels (plus most office items except stationery) from NEBS (500 Main St., Groton, MA 01471).

(3) Books are mailed one of three ways. FIRST CLASS (when the customer insists and pays the difference, maybe 1% of the time), LIBRARY RATE (to libraries!), and FOURTH CLASS/SPECIAL (Books). The post office will give you a rate sheet that explains all. Buy a hand stamp that says FOURTH CLASS/SPECIAL since almost all of your books (or tapes) will be mailed that way.

(4) We simply buy sheets of stamps, tear them up, and mix and match. Stamp machines are fine but expensive and time-consuming. Get a receipt for tax purposes each time you buy the stamps.

(5) Very, very few books fail to arrive. If someone complains we ask them to wait two more weeks and if it still isn't there, let us know. If they do, we send another. If the order to individual clients tops $50, we insure the package for its market value closest to $50 or $100. We ship larger orders to resellers by UPS.

(6) Record every order on a daily tabulation sheet. You must account for the total income received: the amount for the book, product, or service; for tax, and for shipping. Accounts receivable are noted twice: on an A/R sheet when the invoice is typed and sent and on the daily tab sheet when it is paid. The figures on the daily tabulation sheet are then recorded on the income ledger, which we keep by computer. Ultimately the orders, some with credit card receipts, are attached to this sheet and filed should we need to consult any order or the daily tally at some future date.

(7) Keep complete books. Basically you must account for all income and all expenses. Go to a stationery store and buy a general business ledger book. Modify it to meet your needs. You will need an ACCOUNTS RECEIVABLE and INVENTORY section. Just remember to keep all receipts and all orders.

(8) As mentioned earlier, unless you are doing business solely in your name — the Tom Smith Company (and you are Tom Smith) — you

will need to file a fictitious business statement. Check with the County Clerk for details. This must be done before you can open a business bank account.

(9) Visit several banks to check rates and services. Important will be the cost and availability of a Mastercard/VISA service through that bank since many customers will want to buy a book that way. This will be even more important when you have several books or products, where impulse buying of many items is possible.

(10) If you are in a state with a sales tax, you will need to register with that office to get a resale number. Ask any other businessperson who sells products for the address: they are painfully aware of their local taxing group. Be modest in your estimate of the sales you will make at the outset or you may be required to post a bond and pay more frequently than other new businesses. Check locally to see if other licenses are required.

(11) You need a federal tax number only when you hire employees other than your family. Otherwise you report the business on your tax form as a sole proprietorship or partnership.

(12) Keep the full name, title, firm, and address of everybody who inquires by phone (if possible) and by mail. This is your future mailing list. When you write a second book to this targeted market, you send a pre-publication special to these names so they can order at a discounted rate before the book is available to the public. This can result in the printing costs being met before anyone has read a word!

EXAMPLE

Time to let others know that I've prepared and produced (or soon will) a book that they would benefit much from reading. Time to do what I've preached on these pages. Time to promote and sell.

There are 75,000 principals in need of my book! I must get the word to them, by flyer first, then again and again, less expensively, to reinforce the book's existence, validate its worth, and remind them that if they forgot to buy, here's another chance!

You know by now that I do not intend to produce this book for principals but created the model because it requires no special inside information to comprehend and is easy to modify to your field of specialization for a self-published book to your tightly-targeted market.

Nonetheless, let me show you what I would do to promote and market this book. I will create a set of fliers as well, to give you an idea of how the final promotional tools might look, though I'll beg off paying the $1,500 for final, fancy examples and show them to you, rather, in final rough form as I would submit them to a graphic artist (or advertising agency) for technical completion. What is critical here is the thought/action process. Your final tools will be as different as your market requires.

The much-heralded flyer!

Heralded indeed, for this element is the difference, at least in our example and probably for most other TCE books, between sweet success and doleful disaster. That is, prepaid books happily on their way to eager buyers or a mound of books gathering dust, unsold because they are unknown by those who need what they say.

I've tested the book, using a wee portion of the mailing list, and now I must direct my limited finances, as explained in Chapter 10, to sending a flier to every person on that mailing list, 16,750 in the first mailing, the rest of the 58,250 as the books sell to the first responses.

For the flyer, I complete the 10-step checklist that follows to get it prepared, positioned, and in the mail. At the same time I buy shipping supplies, find a working space to fill orders, and set up the personnel and operating logistics of fulfillment. (I've already filed the fictitious business statement, rented a postal box, and contacted the state taxing agency.)

(1) review the copy material from the dummy flyer
(2) make all necessary changes
(3) add new copy (table of contents, biographical information, etc.), including a money-back guarantee or its equal
(4) design the flyer and have the copy typeset
(5) get a PMT of book cover, a recent photo of myself, and have halftones made of them, if needed
(6) prepare the camera-ready boards or hire another to do so
(7) coordinate preparation, printing, and delivery to the mailing house
(8) select and order the best mailing lists, in Cheshire form
(9) determine the number of fliers wanted, when, for whom
(10) arrange mailing and postage with mailing house

I have no example of my final flyer in this book for two very simple reasons: there are hundreds of better examples that I want you to use instead of relying too much on just one. And because I would rather suggest, for your first book (and probably all that follow), that you use professional help at this stage rather than gamble solely on your ability to produce **the** selling flyer. That is, let somebody else prepare the flyer for you.

As for other examples, I want you to gather as many other fliers as you can find and study them. Some you will receive in the mail, others are readily available from libraries, teachers, businesses, and other publishers. Ask the reference or acquisitions librarian to study their "buy" file. While at the library, read the *Publishers' Trade List Annual.* Particularly pay attention to those books being sold to your targeted market.

Getting a professional to help prepare the flyer

From the three ad agencies best prepared to help me, I pick one. I call and make an appointment with the director. I bring my Information Sheet and the items from the 10-step checklist just read.

Then I get some key business done before we look at the copy. Who has experience with direct mail at that agency? May I see examples of the work produced? How did those examples pull? How many items were bought from those mailers? With whom would I work on my project? (If you have no experience with flyer preparation or direct mail, work from the outset with the advertising agency, supplying necessary information and letting them translate that into selling copy.)

If I'm satisfied with the response and believe that the particular person with whom I would work could produce a selling flyer, then we discuss my situation: my book and my market, plus my concept of how to get that market to buy my book as seen in the rough form of the flyer. I need their response and ideas or suggested modifications, plus what it will cost and how long it will take them to complete the finished artwork in camera-ready fashion.

In the meantime I contact medium-sized print shops in the city nearby, check fliers similar to mine that they have recently printed, and get bids for printing my flyer. Included in the printing bid is delivery to the mailing house.

Once the artwork is completed, I take it to the printer. A day or two later I look at the blue lines. The fliers are printed, delivered to the mailing house, and off they go to the principals! All coordinated by a schedule worked out with the ad agency, printer, and mailer. My role is to see that the flyer says what it must say in the best selling manner for my market, that it looks right, and that it is mailed in the proper form and on time.

My promotion and selling campaign beyond the flyer

My earlier market test showed that principals would most likely buy my book by mail, at gatherings, after presentations, or if it were required for a class or certification. I'll save those for the next chapter. They are slow, spotty means. Now I'll concentrate on increasing my mail sales, to build on the awareness the flyer creates.

I'll focus on the two major associations, one each for elementary and secondary school principals, plus five other, smaller associations of principals. (At the same time, I'll gather similar information about superintendents and other top school administrators for possible use later.) I want my book in front of the principals' eyes before, during, and after the fliers are mailed. That means:

(a) a news release about the coming book in each association's publications
(b) a review in each association's publications
(c) a display ad in the largest association publications
(d) an article by me or another person about the book's subject in which my book is mentioned, with price and necessary ordering directions, in as many association publications as possible
(e) perhaps a flyer inserted in the association mailing to its members
(f) inclusion of the book on any association preferred reading list
(g) inclusion of the book in items sold by the association to its members or the public at large
(h) inclusion of the book in any class, seminar, or similar activity of or sponsored by the association

What we need to know next is which of the associations listed in Chapter 4 have publications, how often they publish each year, and to how many subscribers, members, or recipients each issue is sent. Where can I find this information in the library? The *Encyclopedia of Associations* (the information below is from the 1988 edition), with the (*) circulation and additional listings from *Ulrich's International Periodicals Directory*, 1988, and 1987 *Gale Directory of Publications*, (formerly *Ayers Periodical Directory*).

Association-related publications: principals

NASSP (Nat'l Assn of Secondary School Principals); 37,000 members:
Bulletin, 9X yr/38,000* circulation
Newsleader, 9X yr/35,000
Student Activities, 9X yr
Curriculum Report, 5X yr
Legal Memorandum, 5X yr/35,000*
School Tech News, 5X yr
The Practitioner, 4X yr/38,000*
Schools in the Middle, 4X
Administrative Information Report, irregular
*Tips for Principals**, 6X yr/38,000

NAESP (Nat'l Assn of Elementary School Principals); 22,000:
Communicator (newsletter), 10X yr
Principal, 5X yr/23,000*
   also books, handbooks, pamphlets

NATTS (Nat'l Assn of Trade and Technical School Principals); 1,002:
Washington Update, weekly
Newsletter, monthly
Career News Digest, 3-4X yr
Career Training Journal, 3-4X yr
   also handbooks and handouts

National Conference of Yeshiva Principals; 1,000:
Machberes Hamenahel (Principal), monthly/1,000*
Newsletter, monthly
   also curriculum materials

Other association-related publications: superintendents/administrators

AASA (American Assn of School Administrators); 18,000:
The School Administrator, 11X yr
   also books, special reports, pamphlets, audio and video cassettes

AFSA (American Federation of School Administrators); 10,000:
News, 7X yr

NABSE (Nat'l Alliance of Black School Educators); 3,000:
News Brief, irregular

News release

News releases are relatively simple to write, can be sent to all of the publications above, and might find their way into print. The problem is one of timing: I want to have a review of the book appear on those same pages soon after the book is in print.

Most of the association publications are monthly or appear every second month during the school year. That means that the news release should be in their hands at least two months before the actual publication date. Which means to me that the moment I know what my book is about, its title, and I have set an actual print date I should write and mail the news releases.

Simple and direct is the rule here. The shorter, the more likely it is to be slipped into the other copy. An example for my book might look like that on the next page.

A book review

Dan Poynter says it best: "Book reviews are the most effective and least expensive method of promoting your book to the retail market." They are even more effective to tightly-targeted markets, where every reader has a vested interest in reading more about your topic.

There are 21 publications for principals and top educational administrators listed above. Even though I'm certain that most of them don't include book reviews, I don't know which do. A check at two large university libraries has only five of the publications available, and four of them do review books. The rest are obviously smaller; most probably don't. (I could contact each association and ask for a copy of each to be sent to me, of course.) Why take a chance? It costs less than $2 to mail each packet and any lost opportunity could be scores to thousands of copies of my book unsold. So I will send a book review packet to each publication.

I read *The Self-Publishing Manual* and put together my packet: a copy of the book, an information sheet, two sample reviews of the book itself (written by me or another, one a page long, the other, two, both double-spaced in news release format), a cover letter, a reply card, and a sharp b/w photo of the book cover.

NEWS RELEASE

Bassman-Willer Press
P.O. Box 6405
Santa Maria, CA 93456
March X, 19xx
(805) 937-8711

CONTACT: Elmer Wiggins

Release date: May 1, 199X

School principals lead two lives, one academic, the other personal. When the school life becomes all-inclusive, trouble lurks. Finding himself in that trap, the author looked in vain for guidance in print. Nothing. So Gordon Burgett wrote his seventh book, **Principals: How to Find Your Family, Fun, Fire, Fortune, and a Fascinating Future While the Teachers Teach, the Kids Bloom, and the Buildings Bulge!**

"Somewhere around my twelfth year I began to lose identity, then I wondered what was left for me. The school part was fine. It was the 'other me' who was out of kilter," says Burgett, winner of California's prestigious "Distinguished Educator" award in 1987 and a much-sought keynote speaker at education gatherings nationwide.

Burgett hunted for models: principals who lived both lives equally well, whose schools were as exciting as their personal lives were full and challenging. From 26 interviews conducted in all parts of the United States, he has woven their advice into additional research to create a book both practical and humorous for principals at every school level.

Available on May X, 199X, the 200-page paperback is available for $14.95 (plus $1 for shipping) from Bassman-Willer Press, P.O. Box 6405, Santa Maria, CA 93456 or through your school library distributor.

To whom should I send my book review packet? Since most associations farm the book reviews out to members to write, I have no idea who will pass judgment on my masterpiece. Therefore I'll send the packet directly to the editor whose name appears in the most recent issue. (If the publications are unavailable, I can either call the associations for their names or check *Ulrich's International Periodicals Directory*, Volume 3 for the Index, then to Volume 1 for the section on "Education — School Organization and Administration.") While checking this source I also find other groups to which I may wish to send promotional information: state societies, similar groups in Canada and Australia/New Zealand, even the Association of International Education Administrators. I always include the position with the name in case the editor has been replaced.

How might the cover letter and reply card look? The reply card is below; the cover letter, on the next page.

We have received the complimentary copy of the review book or galleys you sent of
_____

[ ] We expect to review this book on the following date:_____
[ ] Please send a photograph of the author.
[ ] We do not intend to review this book because _____

Name of reviewer: _____

Full job title: _____

Name of publication:_____

Mailing address:_____

Comments (optional):_____

_____

Tightly-Targeted Markets

Bassman-Willer Press
P.O. Box 6405
Santa Maria, CA 93456
March X, 19xx

Dear Reviewer:

School principals live in a fishbowl world, trying on the one hand to create and maintain an exemplary school, on the other, an exemplary life. Nobody is more visible in the community than the person doling out discipline, setting an example for faculty and staff, and modelling to students the good things that can come from learning.

Yet they are human too, painfully aware of their frailties. And conscious of the fact that a principalship can quickly become all-absorbing, and that their personal lives, dreams, and out-of-school needs can fade and too often disappear, sometimes with dire consequences.

Finally, a book that addresses the principal's "other life"! Called **Principals: How To Find Your Family, Fun, Fire, Fortune, and a Fascinating Future While the Teachers Teach, the Kids Bloom, and the Buildings Bulge!**, I interviewed 26 principals across the United States to see how the most successful led full, exciting, challenging lives both in and out of their school, then added research and reframed their responses into six main categories, described on the Information Sheet accompanying this letter.

Some 75,000 principals need models of their own. If you agree that the book enclosed would be a valuable reference to most if not all of those 75,000, would you help me make them aware of its existence through a review in your publication? I will be grateful, and so will they.

Respectfully,

Gordon Burgett

Display ads

When might I consider running a display ad in the best of these publications? If they are going to review the book, a display ad near or next to the review might make sense — particularly if the review urges the reader to buy the book! Unfortunately, one never knows what a reviewer will say, particularly a member of the association called upon now and then to pass judgment.

The second occasion that might call for a display ad would be the appearance of an article about the subject by me or another whose angle I know.

The topic will be treated positively and my book will be mentioned so an ad nearby should reinforce the theme and tell readers how they can order more good information about it. This requires coordinating the position of the article and advertisement for maximum benefit.

The third time when I might consider a display ad would be in the issue that the association members would read after they had received my flyer, to add whatever validity and reinforcement being on those august pages might carry. If that advertisement draws a significant increase in orders, I would repeat it again, and keep doing so as long as it brought three times its cost in new orders.

If interested, I'd call the association and speak to the advertising manager of the publication(s) to request that a rate sheet and any other information necessary be sent to me. Similar information can also be found in the library in the appropriate SRDS book.

Alas, my budget is so tight I can't afford to follow my own advice for this book. No display ads this time.

An article or articles about the subject

All that's involved here is time and skill, very little money. Just what the alley catter loves!

Which publications use articles about principals, and which uses the most? The most recent guide I could find was two years old, the Current Index to Journals in Education. Of the approximately 875 journals cited in its index, the greatest number of articles under "principals" were found in:

NASSP Bulletin (published 9 times a year)	13
Theory in Practice (5X year)	11
Principal (5X year)	10
School Administrator (11X year)	4
Educational Administration (4X year)	3
Executive Educator (12X year)	3
Journal of Educational Administration (Australia, 2X year)	3

Other sources I could use to find similar information would be the *Education Index*, with 353 magazines and journals listed; the *Resources in Education*, and (for far more general items) the *Reader's Guide to Periodical Literature*. (Each index includes the address of each publication cited.)

Why is it important to know this? Articles about principals are read by principals, so if I want to get information before that readership, these guides indicate which publications are most likely to do just that, in a priority order.

Four of the seven publications are not from the associations, so that gives me new areas to explore for display ads, certainly for book reviews, and, if needed, for different mailing lists.

How will I handle the articles? That is, how will I know how many to write and which editor is most likely to use my words? By approaching the task like a professional: by querying first, then writing an article only to those who respond positively.

First I'll see if the publication is listed in the current *Writer's Market*. If not, I'll get the editor's name through Ulrich's or by phone. Then I'll send a solid, selling one-page query letter that asks, in essence, "Would you be interested in an article about ...?" The query letter will sell me, through the way it is written, and my subject, by how it brings that alive and makes its importance manifest. If the editor says yes, I will write a customized article for that readership and those pages, drawing from my book and probably mentioning it. The article will be sharp, so interesting any editor will be delighted to have it on his/her pages. Then I'll consider a display ad to run nearby. Finally, I'll discuss with the editor how the address and ordering information can be included in the text or in the bio blurb. But only after the article is accepted.

Could I get someone else to write the article? Sure. They get any payment made for it, which for educational journals would likely be a few free copies. Or I can sweeten the pie a bit, paying them $100, or more, for every article they get placed in a principal-read publication, as long as they mention my book (but only once) in the text. Why would I pay them? Because I should earn far more than that from sales resulting from that exposure. But I won't put their payment on a royalty or per-sale basis because it is too hard to track the source of all my sales to calculate their payment.

And what about a series of articles or a column? Super, in the right publication! A bit more on that in the next chapter, but for now I'll work on writing the best article first. Without that, a series or a column won't happen. The article is the seed.

An insert in the association mailing

There's another way to put my flyer in many principals' hands other than mailing it myself. If the associations would let me include it in their key magazine mailing (or any other mailing that reached all of their members), I could save a considerable amount of money (for the mailing list, handling, and postage) and still reach a large part of my targeted market.

In this case the NASSP and the NAESP, for secondary and elementary school principals, have a combined mailing of 60,000 for their key publications. The advantage is measured in dollars, time and energy saved coordinating the mailing, and the prestige of having the flyer arrive with a valued publication.

The disadvantage would be the 15,000+ principals who would not be reached, using the mailing list rentals as a guide. It would be too costly, if possible at all, to determine which names on the mailing lists were not in the NASSP and NAESP distributions.

I have decided not to pursue this simply because, in this book, I want to describe the other process more fully to you. But should it interest you, start by contacting the best and most obvious mailings to your market to see if they have an insert program in place, and if so would they send information to you about it. (Once again, Standard Rate and Data Services comes to the rescue. In their publication about mailing lists is a section about inserts, with a list and information about tag-along programs seeking participants. Read this in addition to contacting your most obvious carriers.)

If the cost was right (that is, low) I might consider a second mailing to my market about a year after the first, this time through an insert.

Other inclusions

While none of these immediately apply to my topic or the associations per se that would be most directly affected by my book, the prospect of getting my book on a preferred reading list (anybody's!), having it sold by a group to its members or the public at large (any group!), or finding my book included in required or suggested readings for a class, seminar, or like activity (any format!) makes me, or any bookseller, smile. Moreover, the last two will be pursued in detail after mail sales begin to abate. Since sales are the result of having the book in wide circulation and known, my first efforts will be to flood my targeted market, then to work the spillovers later.

Card Deck

I check the SRDS reference and find, to my surprise, a card deck exclusively for principals! Printed twice a year, it is mailed to 100,000+: 77% from public schools and 13% from private (10% parochial).

So I write the card deck producers for a sample copy of the last mailing, which I study in detail to see, should I decide to pursue this secondary promotional technique, what my card should look like.

The sample packet included 36 cards plus one double-fold, four-colored insert. Sixteen had one color only, another 16 had two, and five had four colors. The second colors were red (9), blue (3), magenta (2), yellow (1), and green (1) — all with black the basic color on white card stock. Without a prepaid stamp (but with a space marked "place stamp here") were 16, with a printed prepaid stamp were six. Twelve more were in order form style but had no return face. Three were simply information sheets. Not a one had a principal-only product; all products were school-related. Regarding the value of the product, 6 were in the $1-10 range; 2, $11-20; 7, $20-30; 10, $30+, and 11, unclear. Most of the last urged the principal to send for specific details.

What would it cost to take part in a mailing?

```
  $ 1395
+  100  for a second color on the message side
-    2 % if I pay with the order
+  100  for artwork
  $ 1565.10
```

By selling the book at $14.95 I would have to sell about 104 books through the card deck to break even. Using 100,000 as the distribution total, that would be a buying ratio of .104%, with each card costing $ .015651.

Since my small test market showed 2% would buy the principal's book if they heard about it through card decks, that is far higher than the break-even ratio of .104%. If it is to be fully believed, 2% of this mailing universe would be 2,000 sales and $29,900 in income, although I have no idea of how many who would buy by card deck would also have purchased the book through the direct mail flyer.

What am I going to do? Call ten of those who took part in this last mailing, trying to select those with a product most like mine in content and cost. Ask if it pulled well and would they do it again.

Then make up my own mind. If I decided to add this to my promotional campaign, I would write the copy for the card (mostly drawing from the flyer), have the card typeset front and back, have an overlay prepared (or do it myself) for the second color, mail the artwork and check to the card deck publisher, and get ready to fill orders.

Would I do it? Very likely, with the only negative influence being a strong warning from those who participated in the last mailing. If I see the flags up, I'll check many more than ten before deciding. If I go ahead, it will have to be after the flyer mailing, paying for this from the profits from those sales, using it as a sweeper to remind all principals, this time by card deck, to buy this book they've received a flyer about, seen referred to in their professional journals, and heard lauded by their colleagues. Don't I wish! Billboards, skywriting, Donahue and Carson....

Book Clubs and Premiums

Nothing here. No book clubs for principals only, or that seem really appropriate for this narrow a book. Unfortunately. I'll ask those that cater to the educational field anyway, but without much hope.

And premiums? It seems likely that there would be some group out there trying to sell something that would want to catch the principals' attention and gratitude with such a stellar book, but I sure can't think of any nor could the six principals I spoke with. There was the fear, expressed by them, that by offering this book it might seem like a bribe to stimulate interest in another item that had to be bought. But I will keep my eyes and ears open. I can always produce an update or case study related to this theme, use it later as a premium item, and refer to the book in it, selling the basic text after-the-fact. Intriguing, but for later. A greater intrigue is whether I can get my tightly-targeted market to buy in even greater numbers than I hope by simply putting my flyer directly in their hands.

EXPANDING

The "E" of TCE means "Expanded"

If your targeted market will buy your information in book form to meet a need or solve a problem, why wouldn't they buy that same information by other means? Or more or similar information in another book by you?

Would they pay to attend a seminar to hear more about your topic? Would somebody or some firm or association pay you to give a speech about it? Or could you sell books or other products to those coming to a seminar or speech?

Would they hire you as a consultant, to learn how to apply your information to their personal or corporate needs? Would they buy more information through a newsletter as it becomes available? Would they rather hear the book on audio tapes as they drive? Or see you explain its main points on a video?

Again, what you are selling is expertise. Why sell it once in one form only? Why not take the information gathered while writing your book and share it many ways?

For example, as we saw in Chapter 7, why not produce articles, consult, and offer seminars from the information gathered as you write the book? And from the seminars develop both speeches and tapes? The book, in final form, would yield more articles, and further gathering of related information would provide a basis for a newsletter. The book, in turn, could be sold at the seminars and speeches as well as through consulting and a newsletter.

Expansion from a common information root allows you to multiply manifold both income and exposure, which in turn enhances your position and perception as an expert. It is also far easier and less expensive per item to collectively sell many products by direct marketing to a specific buyership.

Expansion is the reward you get for doing the targeting and customizing right. The rewards can be huge!

15
CONVERTING THE BOOK INTO MORE BOOKS

Once you have written a book you have a core from which many more books can be developed. We set an earlier goal of earning $50,000 from your first book, and suggested that you could probably earn another $50,000, or much more, by expanding from that information base. In this section we will focus on that second $50,000, or more, through additional books. In the next section, through other means.

The spinoff books can be new editions of the original book (changed, updated, or both), they can come from further development of elements introduced in the first (or subsequent) book(s), or they can be books about closely related topics of interest to the same targeted market.

Each successive book is easier to research (you know the sources), easier to produce (you know the process), and easier to sell (you know the buyers).

Best of all, easier to sell. People want more good things from the same good writer. Which is why your first book must be excellent. And why it makes huge sense to go to that same well time and again. (Major publishers know that too. That's why they advance a James Clavell $5,000,000 on an outline of a book. People want to read more from the man who wrote *Shogun* and *King Rat*. Reputation alone assures them that they still clear the $5,000,000!)

Here are 12 ways to turn your first book into many more. (This list isn't definitive. Find other ways that apply to your topic and knowledge.)

(1) The most obvious: every three years or so you go back to the same book, update and expand it, include new quotes, review new research, add new sources to the bibliography....

(2) Write a time-dated book: *Dentists: How To Save 50% on Your 1989 Income Tax*. Next year is 1990, and so on.... Look at the tax prep books in the bookstore. But it needn't be taxes. It can be car models, computers, where to find current cancer research, the National League pennant race, and many more.

(3) Write a many-pronged book. *Five Things Every Successful C.P.A. Needs To Know*. That's the first book. Each of those five things is the core of the next five books.

(4) Write the follow-up to the many-pronged book, also many-pronged. *Ten More Things Crucial to Successful Accounting.* And, you guessed it, each of those ten is the core of the next ten books.

(5) Focus on stages of importance to the targeted market, beginning with any stage and filling out the cycle with subsequent books. An example of such a cycle: (a) *How To Form Your Own Band*, (b) *How To Double the Number and Value of Your Paid Gigs*, (c) *How To Multiply Your Band Income Through Product Sales*, (d) *How To Get Your Band Taped, Recorded, Played, and Rich!*, (e) *How To Take Your Band National!*

(6) Having become identified with a core topic by writing about it, gather all the other writing about that or directly-related topics and prepare an anthology. Most of this writing will already be in print as articles, reports, or studies. Additional material could be prepared by you or others in the field specifically for this anthology. You are the editor; if you also contribute you are both editor and a co-author (with one or many).

(7) Produce a book of comic relief. Unless you are extraordinarily gifted in a comedic way, this will be an anthology of jokes, cartoons, quips, anecdotes, humorous excerpts, whatever makes the targeted market laugh. These can be gift books for those in the field to give each other or for those outside the field to give to the insiders. In the latter case your marketing must be expanded and approached differently.

(8) Use case studies for books. A book could be one case study or a dozen clustered around the same point or theme. These could also be produced in booklet rather than book form. You could write them, co-author, or publish the case studies of others.

(9) A source book is a natural since you are already familiar with the main texts and how the targeted market might use additional information. Such a book is really an extended, annotated bibliography plus a listing of all additional resources: experts, agencies, speakers in the field, keycollege or university departments, current research and researchers, money fonts, etc. The contents must be accurate and current. Use a computer data search through a major library. Particularly salable if the information and sources are problem/solution based.

(10) A how-to, step-by-step action guidebook which addresses one problem and provides one or various solutions. This would be a good match to a more general first book that broadly covers the field.

(11) Here you can use virtually any of the previous ten but alter the targeted market and the related facts, where appropriate. There are topics where the basic information is roughly the same whether given to a salesperson, a minister, a welder, or a banjo player. Even the presentation format requires little change. So here you find what is different for the new targeted market, adjust and verify those changes, and produce a book either about the original topic or one of the deviations above.

(12) In this spinoff category you zero in on the buyers of your first book. You have their attention and many of their names; you know how to order and use their mailing list. So here you ask what other need do they have that is as pressing as that chosen for your first book. Then you write a book about that new need. If they have many pressing needs, you have many potential books — or one or several books about various needs. Given the opportunity I would respond both to the urgency of the need and its proximity to your first topic, moving from that most closely related to the first book to that least related, attempting to build on the expertise displayed about the topic in that first book.

Incidentally, you needn't write all or any of the spinoff books. Rather, you can use your knowledge of the buying market and the prestige of having written the first book to become a publisher for those who follow. Publishers run the risk but earn the lion's share of the profits. Writer/publishers earn even more.

There are two main points here regarding book expansion. The first: since you have established your expertise with your targeted market about a particular subject, you build from that strength, moving slowly outward and deeper so that everything you do further enhances that perceived expertise. The second: you focus on a pattern or process and you apply that to many markets. From *Lawyers: How To Maximize Your Earning Potential* to *Doctors:...*, *Faculty: ...*, *Truck Drivers: ....*

Of the two, the first will almost always be less risky and more profitable. It is simply easier to sell one person many good things than many people one good thing. The main difference, to your coffers, is the greater ease and lower cost of promotion.

EXAMPLE

Twelve ways to multiply my book for principals

How might I turn my book for principals into a true empire of earnings while helping those badgered souls lead even better, more exciting, and more rewarding lives? Let me respond by adhering to the 12 examples suggested for the general TCE process.

(1) I could update and revise my book every few years, adding some new examples and modestly changing the basic text. Or I could write BOOK 2 and perhaps even BOOK 3 using the same basic theme but totally changing the examples and contents. One source for these additions might be suggestions made by readers. If I stick to the same theme but include completely new support information, I could sell the original book plus each subsequent edition simultaneously.

(2) A year-based change is inappropriate here but other modifications might be considered

> (a) state-by-state or region-by-region, on the assumption that what principals do out of school in California may be different from what they do in, say, Ohio or Alabama
> (b) at various levels: grade school, middle school, and high school principals
> (c) by sex: male principals and female principals
> (d) by the type of school: principals from public schools, religious schools, and private schools
> (e) by location of school: principals from schools that are urban, suburban, or rural

There are two obvious problems that come from dividing the target market into sub-markets: (a) research can be expensive in terms of travel and time, and (b) the selling universe is smaller.

(3) The book I have developed thus far has five sub-divisions: family, fun, fire, fortune, and future. The ideal is to write the basic book, then a spinoff book for each of the sub-topics, exploring them in depth, with many

examples. The main benefit of this approach is clear: I continue to sell more good information to a buyership that already bought (and presumably liked) the first book. I have their names or know where to find them on a mailing list, I can note each of the other books for sale on the same promotional tool or in each subsequent book, and I stay close to the fonts of my original research, moving out from the core. An excellent economy of time, energy, and capital.

(4) A switch here because I may well cover each of the four spinoffs in its own book about as fully as any principal would want. Instead of more ways to find a "full" life for principals, I might redirect that whole, balanced, invigorated person to create the best school possible! There could be dozens of books here. Some titles that first come to mind: *The Principal and the School Board, The Principal and the Community, The Principal and the Faculty, The Principal and the Staff.* You get the idea. Punchy sub-titles might make these books seem even more inviting!

(5) In addition to writing about the principalship from the wholeness aspect, I might explore it from its developmental stages. That might result in books like *How To Become a School Principal, What The Principal Does and How to Do it Better, From Principal to Superintendent, Principals: Getting Ready for Retirement,* and *After You've Rung the Last Bell!* Of these, only the first falls outside of my marketing sphere.

(6) Others are writing about principals and principalship. I can pull those writings together to produce an anthology by gathering articles from other publications and getting required permissions and releases, having the article rewritten, or simply extending the opportunity to those in the field or knowledgeable about it to write specifically for an anthology. I select the topic, probably write the first chapter and introductory material for each component, perhaps add new segments, and publish this for the same market that bought my original book. The themes can either be the spinoffs discussed in (3) or more directly tied to the school, as suggested in (4) and (5).

(7) Comic relief! This can be specifically about principals, if that much material exists, or can be broader, touching all elements involved in the principal's life: school, kids, teachers, playground, superintendent, parents, board of education, supplies, buses, staff, etc. If cartoons and artwork are done in easy-to-copy fashion, I'll be sure to mention my book and how it can be bought (price, where to order) with each cartoon or item. Therefore,

when it's copied and sent to friends my book selling information also has a chance of being copied and sent! I might even ask the buyer: "If you make copies of ... please do us (and the recipient) a favor by including the source. They may want a copy of their own!"

(8) Case studies would be very appealing to principals, particularly if they are problem-oriented and contain detailed means of resolving those problems. A slightly different tack: let's say the theme is "Goals and Teamwork." I find, say, six examples of schools where the principal was the motivating spirit in setting up exemplary programs. The ideal would be to go to each school, gather information, and write up all six myself. Next, it would be to have that principal (or somebody designated) write it up, with me providing key points to touch so that all case studies have shared points of comparison. All six would be combined in one case study.

The case studies would be no-nonsense reports: what is the purpose, how it is being met, what works, what doesn't, how it could be improved, and recommendations. There is a demand for as many hard-hitting, fact-filled case studies as there are problems.

(9) Like the case studies, there are areas where information is needed but scattered and tedious to assemble. Principals need access to information to initiate change or justify action; so do boards of education and superintendents. Examples leap to mind: school or district consolidation, student rights (dress, freedom through student publications, retention, punishment), funding, firing....

This book would be topic-based, a compilation of all printed information, with the most important included, the rest cited in an annotated bibliography. It might include statutes, law cases, job descriptions, operations manuals, the names of experts in the field, and much more.

(10) Rather than just sources (although they would be included), this book would provide step-by-step directions on how to solve problems that all or most principals face. Or it might include steps followed by, say, five principals, much like the case study book. Five organizational steps might be (a) the problem defined, (b) possible solutions, (c) examples where these solutions have been tried, (d) steps most likely to provide a solution to the reader, (e) sources of additional information and assistance.

(11) Here I want to build on the research I have but for a different market. So the question is, "What other people or groups have needs similar to principals?" Four come to mind: superintendents, members of the school board, athletic directors, and teachers.

For superintendents the out-of-school life is similar and the need to focus on it, much the same. So I can either rewrite the book, adjusting the facts to fit superintendents; I can write to both principals and superintendents from the outset, carrying both in the title and text, or I can promote the book for principals to superintendents, stressing the high percentage of overlap of need.

For school boards and athletic directors, the school-related books I write might well be rewritten, and factually adjusted, for those markets.

As for teachers, a reworking of the book would be necessary. This is a potentially huge market, whether written for teachers at a grade level or by subject. As mentioned earlier, I could even write a book for parents of students at a certain grade! *How Your Child Can Excel in Fifth Grade!* or *Helping Your Fifth Grader Love Learning!* or something of that nature. Anybody who has kids will have a fifth grader at some point. And if they buy a great book about fifth grade, why wouldn't they buy one for every grade?

(12) Principals are book-oriented, active, inquisitive people. They have interests beyond school (which is what our first book addresses), at the school, and in living in general. Are there other books I could write to them that we haven't suggested above? Sure. What about *Principals and Their Own Kids: a How-To Love Book?* Or a *Making Sense of Being in Charge* book. Or a dozen others that nibble at the corners of their dreams, duties, and life.

16 SHARING THE INFORMATION BY OTHER DISSEMINATION MEANS

Not everybody wants to read a book, and not all information is best conveyed that way. Teaching the movement of a particular ballet, for example, might be done on paper, but video tape is better. Martin Luther King's speeches read well; seen or heard, they gain immense strength and they teach more. Interactive seminars defy capture on paper; the medium is molded while the information is shared.

So the question here is how the core of your book can be shared again, as is or restructured, by other means of dissemination. How it can be remarketed through articles, speeches, seminars, tapes, a newsletter, consulting....

Moreover, how you can reap even higher profits from research now completed and expertise established in a tested target market.

Alas, the concept and process of taking information and forming and packaging it profitably by many means would take a full book to explain well. Good fortune! That's precisely what my previous book does: *Empire-Building by Writing and Speaking*.

Since the theme of this book is "self-publishing," let me refer you to *Empire-Building* for a detailed explanation, share three basic steps now by which you might expand your book into other means, and lightly apply these three to the example, the principals, in the next section:

(1) Complete a fact chart about the subject and means.

(2) Identify the most appropriate means and prioritize those to create action paths.

(3) Extract, again prioritize, and put into a time frame those actions most likely to earn the highest profit. Thus, develop an action plan.

EXAMPLE

Your book for your market (symbolically expressed here as my book to principals) is what this book is about: primarily what we do before we prepare, publish, and promote, and how every step then and thereafter is consistent with a larger plan to meet a vital need of a particular, chosen people.

My focus on these pages has been to show you how you can create and sell a book to meet that need, and how that can bring you much personal satisfaction and, for having taken the dare and met the challenge, much profit.

In Chapter 7 I suggested that sharing needed information doesn't stop with the book, nor do the profits. In the beginning of this chapter I direct you to *Empire-Building by Writing and Speaking*, another text that addresses this spinoff process fully. I do that not to sell more of my books — it sells very well on its own, thank you — but because it is the only such book written. And because, though it falls outside the purview of "self-publishing," you must know about it.

But rather than simply send you elsewhere, which would irk me if I were first reading these words, let me show you how I might have developed some action paths, then an action plan for the book about principals, so you at least get a sense of the full range of ways the information can be spread and how the book, in this case, plays such a central role.

A fact chart about the subject and means

To evaluate and compare the ways by which I might share more information about improving the principals' personal lives beyond the book, I develop a rather simple subject/means chart. I list the means of information dissemination most applicable down the left and the questions I want answered atop columns to the right, as seen in this example:

Subject/Means Fact Chart

Subject: _____

	Exist? In use now?	Where hear about? or see them?	Likelihood of use?	How much do they pay now?	Maximum they might pay?
Means:					
Article					
Book					
Talk					
Speech					
Seminar					
Tape, A-C					
Tape, V-C					
Newsletter					
Consulting					

For articles, for example, I want to know if someone else is already writing about the topic, where they would read about it (that is, in what kinds of publications would these articles appear), how likely would the editor be to want such information on his/her pages, what is the pay range of those publications, and anything else that will help me later decide whether that means is worth pursuing.

Where is this information coming from? Wherever I can find it. I must dig it out. Which means time and energy. Specifically, I will comb the *Reader's Guide to Periodical Literature*, the education indexes, the current *Writer's Market*, and the most likely magazines for principals. I might make some phone calls or write some pre-query letters to editors. Whatever is needed to get a handle on this as a means by which I can share information, earn money, and perhaps sell more books in the doing.

There is another kind of subject/means fact chart — there are as many, I suppose, as you can think up — that works quicker for me. It looks like this:

Another Kind of Subject/Means Fact Chart

Subject: _____

	$ Costs	Time Costs	Expected Income Results
Means:			
Article			
Book			
Talk			
Speech			
Seminar			
Tape, A-C			
Tape, V-C			
Newsletter			
Consulting			

It asks (1) how much would this means cost me in cash, (2) how much in time, and (3) what can I expect to earn from it?

What follows is that second chart filled in, with some means excluded because I felt they were impractical, totally unprofitable, or inapplicable:

Subject/Means Fact Chart for Principal Book

Subject: _____

Article

Cost in dollars: research, preparation, mailing = $25/article
Cost in time: if from book material, 2-5 hours rewrite plus 2 hours to market
    and mail = 4-7 extra hours
Expected income results: $0-250 possible, plus bio plug and expertise
    display; book reference should sell 5-300 copies each article

Tightly-Targeted Markets

Column

Cost in dollars: same as article = $10/column
Cost in time: 2-4 extra hours
Expected income results: $10-50/article possible, plus excellent name display; book reference should sell 10-20 books per column

Speech

Cost in dollars: research, preparation of script and introduction, marketing letter, brochure/flyer, preparation of audio-visual items = $50-1,000
Cost in time: research, write script, practice, write/produce/mail letter/flyer/A-V, marketing = 20-150 hours
Expected income results: talks = no income but good exposure for book, seminar, consulting; speech = $100-1,000

Seminar

Cost in dollars: research, preparation of script/workbook, marketing letter, preparation of audio-visual items, BOR items = $150 + $1.50 each participant workbook
Cost in time: research, write script/workbook, practice, marketing, produce A-V and BOR items = 30-50 hours
Expected income results: $250-850 per seminar, plus BOR sales; add $7 per person if book is a required purchase. Excellent exposure for consulting and speeches

Newsletter

Cost in dollars: access to contributors, books and magazines, journals; association membership(s); computer; pasteup tools or Pagemaker/laser printer; modem; distribution facilities; licenses, etc. = $800-10,000
Cost in time: extremely time-consuming: 6 hours per page for copy prep, editing, research, proofing, typesetting, composition, layout, pasteup, print, fold, mail; 3 hours per page for all business functions of publishing/promotion = 9 hours per page
Expected income results: $2-6/issue per subscriber, plus ad income. Sales vehicle for own book, products, services. Excellent regular display of expertise. Best as adjunct service after other product development.

Consulting

Cost in dollars: telephone, answering service/machine, stationery = $150
Cost in time: time to consult/travel, required preparation and follow-up = varies by client
Expected income results: $50-100/hour. Good contact for later speaking/writing and subsequent consulting

Using the articles columns again, I estimate that on an average it would cost me $25 per article for research, preparation, and mailing. Inexpensive because I have done the book research already and would simply have to draw from that what I'd need to match the slant of the piece. The article examples could come from the pool of book examples already on hand.

Not so inexpensive in terms of time, though, for each article would have to be handcrafted, edited, and fine-tuned: about 4-7 hours, more if the article goes much beyond the book's range.

Is the yield, the income, worth the time, cost, and effort? Not if I'm basing it on what the editor will pay me. Many articles about principals would go to the association and other professional journals or magazines, which means no money. At most I might earn $50-250 from a paying magazine. But in terms of the books sold, that could result, in a conservative estimate, anywhere from $37 to $2,250, figuring the profit at $7.50 each. One hundred sales would be my guess from each article, if the ordering information and cost appear, or $750. Subtract costs and that's a worthy return.

Do the same to all of the means and you get a clear picture: here the best profit comes from the book itself, with sparse pickings from other means. The problem is the subject and the market: a general life topic and principals. If it had been a corporate market or a subject that the buyer felt stronger about, the spinoff money would, therefore, have been greater.

Possible action paths

I've looked at ways to use my book as the core of more books. And now as the hub of related dissemination means. From that I must pick and choose to form cohesive action paths. And I must estimate how much I think I might earn in profits from those paths. What do I get?

Tightly-Targeted Markets

Plan 1:	Book: Principal and Life Outside of School	$ 50,000
	Book 2	40,000
	Book 3	30,000
		$ 120,000
Plan 2:	Book: Principal and Life Outside of School	$ 50,000
	4 additional books: each about one of the four elements of first book, combining fortune/future: $30,000 @	120,000
		$ 170,000
Plan 3:	Book: Principal and Life Outside of School	$ 50,000
	Book: Fifth Grade Teachers	60,000
	Book: Parents of Fifth Graders	15,000-75,000
		$ 125,000-185,000
Plan 4:	Book: Principal and Life Outside of School	$ 50,000
	Book 2	40,000
	6 articles	600
	10 speeches	3,000
	Newsletter ($3 profit 6x yr, 500 subscribers, minus $3,000 for starting costs)	6,000
		$ 99,600

Still, paths are paths, and because they are there doesn't mean they take you where you want to go — or that you will ever follow them. From them you must forge a plan, one that combines the best of the paths (or is the best path) and takes you where you want to go.

There are seven variables that must be considered when you convert an action path into an integrated action plan:

(1) your interest, available time, and energy
(2) how it fits into your general life goals and needs
(3) your financial resources and their accessibility for investment now
(4) the cost of each element — time and expenses — for each means
(5) the success of your initial book
(6) the interest of your targeted market in using the means, plus its ability and desire to pay for the product or service, and
(7) the availability of the information you wish to share

An action plan

You've stuck with me this far, you deserve an action plan!

Prudence tells me to grab PLAN 4 and run with it: $99,600 for two books, six articles, 10 speeches, and a newsletter for one year, with potential big profits forever from that last font.

Its time factors appeal to me too. Figuring the first book at 8-10 months to complete, about 6-8 months for the second, with articles and speeches done during that period, I could work that into an already busy schedule. I'd test the newsletter when the second book was well along, and should there be insufficient interest I could go with Book 3 or any or all of the five books that focus on the ways that principals could enrich their personal lives.

But I've been honest with you throughout this book. I may as well spill the beans now. I'd personally bite on PLAN 3 and chew it into one big meal: learn my trade with the book for principals, then head right for the fifth grade teachers, then the parents. Or some grade and some parents. I liked the idea from the moment I stumbled on the fact, saw how well it fit into the TCE concept, and realized how little has been done that way about such a vital subject.

I love a gamble and plowing into a publishing field where others haven't been is putting your last penny on the line! PLAN 4 is for you if the mere thought of risk makes you quake. PLAN 3 I commend to those who like to roll the dice, even though with TCE they are your dice, fixed your way, on your turf....

A last thought

There is no such thing as totally safe publishing. It's always a gamble. But there are ways to make sharing of information through a book safer, more profitable, less labyrinthian, and much more helpful to people who desperately need your help. That's what I've tried to share with you on these pages. We need to know what you have to say. And you should be rewarded for saying it. So go to it!

BIBLIOGRAPHY

The best books I know about this subject

There are two excellent books that describe, step-by-step, the self-publishing process:

(1) Dan Poynter, *The Self-Publishing Manual* (Para Publishing, revised edition, 1986), $14.95.
(2) Tom and Marilyn Ross, *The Complete Guide to Self-Publishing* (Writer's Digest Books, 1987), $19.95.

Alas, they do not focus on the tightly-targeted market but rather on how the self-publisher can do, on a smaller scale, what larger publishers do for general markets. Highly recommended for information about book production and general book promotion.

In producing the actual book one area often requires guidance: layout and pasteup. The best book I can find for both the beginner and those already experienced in this field is:

(4) Walter Graham, *Complete Guide to Pasteup* (Dot Supply, third edition, 1987), $19.95.

As mystical to newcomers in the publishing field is how to deal with printers. Here I highly recommend the following book, which explains "how to work with printers and graphics arts services to assure quality, stay on schedule, and control costs":

(5) Mark Beach, Steve Shepro, and Ken Russon, *Getting It Printed* (Coast to Coast Books, 1986), $29.50.

Often it is necessary to hire out services to make your book a reality. Sometimes this is done informally. Other times explicit written contracts are more appropriate. An inexpensive way to prepare those contracts is to select from 22 model contracts on disk, enter the numbers appropriate to your situation, make any slight alterations needed, and print out your own agreement ready for signature. The best in this category is:

(6) Dan Poynter and Charles Kent, *"Publishing Contracts"* (Para Publishing,1987), $29.95. Available for MS-DOS and CPM; IBM and many others. Stipulate your computer software with order.

An excellent, new legal guide as valuable to self-publishers as it is to writers attempting to sell their copy to other editors and publishers is:

(7) Brad Bunnin and Peter Beren, *The Writer's Legal Companion* (Addison-Wesley, 1988), $14.95.

Central to TCE publishing is direct mail marketing. Two things help mightily here: common sense and knowledge. I can't help much if you have none of the former, but in this topic I can show you how to gain much of the latter quickly and in an easy-to-comprehend fashion. The best of the lot I think is the following book, just released in the fourth edition:

(8) Bob Stone, *Successful Direct Marketing Methods* (NTC, fourth edition, 1988), $29.95.

Still, there are many, many ways to sell a TCE book other than direct mail, plus ways to increase the number you do sell by direct mail through other means. Poynter and Ross talk about these in their self-publishing books, but the book I find most helpful is:

(9) John Kremer, *1001 Ways To Market Your Books* (Ad-Lib Publications, 1989), $14.95.

Finally, the "E" of TCE means "expanded," and talks about selling the same basic information by other means of dissemination, such as seminars, speeches, articles, tapes, newsletters, consulting, etc. My books, seminars, and tapes deal directly with those means. One book, however, addresses the larger topic of expansion and thus provides the greater framework into which TCE sits. It is called:

(10) Gordon Burgett, *Empire-Building by Writing and Speaking* (Communication Unlimited, 1987), $12.95.

INDEX

Articles, 10, 22, 61, 65-8, 70-5, 78-80, 91, 111, 159, 169, 180, 188, 190-1, 194
Associations, 17, 31, 39-40, 61, 84, 118-9, 169-71, 175-7
Audio cassettes, 10, 61, 65-6, 69, 73-4, 180, 188, 190-1
Award, 91
Benefits, 88, 92, 95-6
Binding, 152
Blue lines, 149, 152, 168
Book clubs, 82, 91, 104, 117, 159, 179
Book list, 91
Book proposal, 12
Book quality, 17
Bookstore(s), 17, 21, 81, 85, 91, 157-8
Booth sales, 22, 81, 85, 104, 160
BOR sales, 72, 80
Brochures (see flyer)
Brokers, mailing list, 29
Buyback, 116-7
Card catalog, 50
Card decks, 22, 91, 160, 178-9
Camera-ready boards, 23, 150-1
Catalogs, 22, 29, 91, 161
Chains, distribution, 17, 21
Charts, 100
Classes, 65-6, 69, 74, 81, 86, 91, 104, 171
Classified ads, 160-1
Co-authorship, 141
Columns, 67, 72, 74-5, 78-80, 192
Commissioned sales representatives, 161
Computer, 99-100, 105, 153-4
Computer software, 65, 74
Consulting, 10, 65, 73-5, 79, 180, 188, 190-2
Contract, book, 13, 116
Conventions, 17, 22, 29, 39, 80-3, 85, 89, 104
Copyright, 113, 119, 123, 137-8, 144
Cost, book, 92
Cover, 99, 106, 108, 119, 129, 152
Cover artist, 155-6
Direct mail marketing, 21-2, 81-2, 85, 91, 158, 162-4, 169

Display ads, 17, 21, 39, 61, 89, 104, 111, 160, 169, 174-5
Distributors, 21
Editing, 135-6, 144
Empire, 20, 71
Expert(ise), 10-11, 53, 62, 91, 132, 154, 180
Film, 69, 74
"Flaming arrow," 19
Flyer, 23, 73, 86, 89, 91-2, 94, 100, 102, 109-11, 158, 161-4, 167-9
Fulfillment, 101-2, 108, 157, 164-6
Garage sales, 81, 86
Illustrations, 23, 92, 94, 99, 103, 107-8, 131-2, 136-7, 141, 151, 155-6
Information sheet, 119, 124-6
Inserts, 160, 177
Interviews, 63, 133, 142-3, 149
Invoice, 23
ISBN, 146, 153
Jobs, 33
Journals, 17, 22, 45, 89, 192
Libraries, 17, 21, 23, 29, 33, 40, 50-1, 57, 60, 68, 73, 81, 86, 91, 141, 157-8
Magazines, 31, 45, 132
Mailing list(s), 26, 29, 31, 33, 37-8, 61, 118, 124, 163
Membership list, 31
Newsletters, 10, 17, 21, 29, 31, 39, 61, 65, 68, 71-4, 78-9, 89, 188, 190-2, 194
Newspapers, 45, 66, 75, 89, 132, 157
News release, 91, 171-2
Novel, 12
Outline, 12, 55, 90, 115, 122, 124
Overhead, 105, 108
Payment rates, book, 13
Payment schedule, 13-4, 16
Permission to quote letter, 138-9, 144
Postage, 101-2
Premiums, 179
Presentations, 83, 169
Price testing, 120
Principal(s), 32, 37-8, 40, 45-8, 57-8, 60-3, 67, 74-80, 85-6, 93, 95-7, 105, 110-1, 120-30, 140-5, 166-79, 184-7, 189-95

Printers, 152, 154
Printing costs, 100, 103, 107-9
Production costs, 98-9, 101-3, 148
Promotion costs, 100, 108
Proofing, 135, 144
Purpose statement, 54, 57, 61-2, 64, 70, 79, 90, 96, 131, 140
Qualifications, TCE, 26, 32-3
Query letter, 12, 14, 17, 80, 111, 15, 133, 190
Questionnaire letter, 126-7
Questionnaire, test, 128
Radio, 13, 65-6, 69, 71, 74, 91, 157, 161
Reference/resource sheet, 13, 115, 122
Releases, 151
Reply card, 120
Reports, 65-6, 68, 71-2, 74-5, 78-9
Research, 12-3, 51-3, 59, 71, 73, 79, 90, 92, 99, 105, 108, 131, 142-3
Reviews, 17, 21, 61, 84, 89, 91, 104, 118, 157, 159, 169, 171, 173-4
Royalties, 13-7, 20, 115-6
Sample chapter, 13
Schools, 17
Secondary questions, 55-7, 62, 64, 71, 79, 90, 131
Seminars/workshops, 65-6, 69-75, 78-81, 83, 86, 89, 91, 104, 117, 123, 161, 169, 177, 180, 188, 190-2
Shipping, 100, 107-8, 117
Shrinkwrap, 108
Speeches, 65-8, 72-5, 77, 83, 88, 91, 104, 123, 161, 180, 190-2, 194

Standard publishing, 12-21, 99, 113-8, 120, 122-3, 130, 157
Subject, 12, 42-5, 48, 52-3, 59, 73
Submission schedule, 13
Subscriber list, 31
Superintendent, 39, 46, 57-8, 76, 78, 80, 95, 169, 170-1
Supermarket, 17
Synopsis, 13, 115
Table of contents, 5, 13, 92, 131
Talks, 65, 67, 71-2, 74-5, 77, 80, 83, 86, 104, 110, 190
Tax, 101-2, 105, 108
Teachers, 40, 45, 57, 61, 76, 104
TCE, 17-8, 20-2, 24, 26, 29, 32, 41, 49-50, 57, 65, 73-4, 82-4, 87-9, 91, 98, 104, 120, 147, 157-8
TV, 13, 65, 66, 69, 74, 91, 157, 161
Telephone solicitation, 104
Testimonials, 53, 61, 92, 132, 141, 149-50, 158-9
Test marketing, 113, 122-9
Textbook, 17, 91
Title, 59, 92, 97, 112-3, 119-22, 128, 131
Topic-spoking, 67-8
Typesetting, 101, 103, 106-8, 149-50, 154
Vertical files, 51
Video cassettes, 61, 65-6, 69-70, 74, 190-1
Word-of-mouth, 17
Working question, 54-5, 57, 62, 64, 71, 79, 90, 115, 131
Working schedule, 64
Writing, book, 15, 23, 90, 92, 134, 143-4

Also available from
COMMUNICATION UNLIMITED

BOOKS

Self-Publishing to Tightly-Targeted Markets	$ 14.95
Empire-Building by Writing and Speaking (paper)	12.95
Empire-Building by Writing and Speaking (cloth)	15.95
Query Letters/Cover Letters	9.95
Speaking For Money (paper)	9.95
Speaking For Money (cloth)	12.95
How To Sell 75% of Your Freelance Writing	9.95
Ten Sales From One Article Idea	7.95

TAPES
(Series with workbooks)

Writing Travel Articles That Sell (180 minutes)	39.95
Writing Comedy Greeting Cards That Sell (120 min.)	24.95
Before You Write Your Nonfiction Book (180 min.)	39.95
How To Set Up and Market Your Own Seminar (180 min.)	44.95

(Single 60-minute tapes)

Finding Ideas for Articles That Sell	9.95
Research: Finding Facts, Quotes, Anecdotes	9.95
How To Be Quoted (Almost) All the Time	9.95
Back-of-the-Room Sales	9.95
Producing and Selling Your Own Audio-Cassettes	9.95

Tax: California residents, add 6% sales tax
Shipping: $1, first book, tape, or series; 50 cents each additional to $2.50 maximum (in U.S.A.)

COMMUNICATION UNLIMITED
P.O. Box 6405
Santa Maria, CA 93456
(805) 937-8711